Coexistence among Human Societies and Ecosystems.

The Geopolitical Elimination of the Common Lands and its Effects on Our Present Global Condition.

From Nature to the Artificial Simulacrum World

Coexistence among Human Societies and Ecosystems.

The Geopolitical Elimination of the Common Lands and its Effects on Our Present Global Condition.

From Nature to the Artificial Simulacrum World

João Pedro GALHANO ALVES

Preface by Farid Benhammou (France)
Preface by Soumaïla Mordia Wali (Niger)

GenNext Publication

Published by

GenNext Publication
5, Ansari Road
Daryaganj, New Delhi-110002
Phone: 011-47034999, 9811692060
E-mail: gennextpublication@hotmail.com

Distribution Network
gyanbooks.com
India, USA, Canada, UK, Australia, France

ISBN: 978-93-5663-139-7 (E-book)

First Published, 2023

Printed at: Gyan Press, Delhi.

Coexistence among Human Societies and Ecosystems.
The Geopolitical Elimination of the Common Lands and its Effects on Our Present Global Condition.
From Nature to the Arti icial Simulacrum World

Author: João Pedro GALHANO ALVES

1st edition in English : © João Pedro Galhano Alves (2009). *"The artificial simulacrum world. The geopolitical elimination of communitary land use and its effects on our present global condition"*. New York (NY, USA) : Eloquent Books, 71 pages.

1st edition in Portuguese : © (all countries except Portugal and Brazil) João Pedro Galhano Alves (2021). *"O mundo de simulacro artificial. A eliminação geopolítica do uso comunitário da terra e os seus efeitos na nossa presente condição global"*. Lisboa (Portugal) & São Paulo (Brazil) : Lisbon International Press, 110 pages.

1st edition in French : © (except in French) João Pedro Galhano Alves (2023). *"Coexistence des sociétés humaines avec des écosystèmes. Les terres communautaires, leur élimination et ses conséquences"*. Paris (France) : L'Harmattan, 142 pages.

2nd edition in English : © João Pedro Galhano Alves (2023). *"The geopolitical elimination of common lands and its effects on our present global condition. From Nature to the artificial simulacrum world"* (e-book). New Delhi (India) : Gyan Books.

Each new edition was reviewed, increased and actualised.

Contents

"We need a new process of development" - Doctor Anil Agarwal, New Delhi, Bharat / India, years 1990.

"What we need is a process of subdevelopment" - Professor José Luis Salinas, Montpellier, France, years 2000.

Abstract

A conjugation of large travels, academic studies, and a career as scientific researcher on anthropology, human cultures, ecology, and political sciences..., allowed João Pedro Galhano Alves to live in some of the rare regions of the Planet, in three continents, where human societies still coexist with ecosystems in state of total or high biodiversity. The comparation of these societies with the techno-industrial societies of mass production and consumption, in state of minimal biodiversity, lead the author to formulate the analysis and concepts contained in this book.

In this book, the author shows the social and ecologic advantages of the communitarian systems for the use of land and natural resources. He describes the historical and geopolitical ways that conducted to their almost total elimination at a global scale, and he analyses the effects, demonstrating how humans evolved during the last millenniums, to reach their present deplorable condition, of mass dependency, production and consumption.

This in-deep study of the systems of property and use of land allows the reader to understand by which reasons the present global ecologic and socioeconomic crises need a change in the social systems of use and management of the territories and natural resources.

This book was published first in English, in New York, NY, USA (2009), after in Portuguese in Lisbon, Portugal and São Paulo, Brazil (2021), and after in French, in Paris, France (2023). Now this work of synthesis, reviewed and actualized, is again published in English, in New Delhi, Bharat / India, as an e-book (2023), for that large Indian and global public have access to its rich thinking contains.

About the author

João Pedro GALHANO ALVES is born in Porto, Portugal, Iberian Peninsula, Europe, in 1962.

He achieved 12 years of Post-Doctorates in Anthropology, Ethnobiology and Ethnology (in France, Spain and Portugal, simultaneously).

This book of Political Anthropology and Ecology, and about the History of land property, was one of the objectives of these Post-Doctorates.

He is also Doctor on Anthropology (France), is Master of Science of High Studies on Agrarian Policies and Administration of the Development (France), he achieved a Diploma of Post-Universitary Specialization (DSPU) on Rural Development (France), and is Agricultural Engineer (Portugal).

He also studied Biologic Agriculture (Portugal), and Agricultural Structures in the Mediterranean Countries (France and Turkey).

During more than three decades, he developed a multidisciplinary research field, about the coexistence of human societies with humanized ecosystems in state of Total or High Biodiversity (concepts defined by him). This means that these ecosystems conserve intact their functional structure, with large territories of wild vegetation, together with agricultural and forestry areas (primary photosynthetic production), and large and stable populations of large wild carnivores (he studied the tiger, the wolf and the lion), secondary consumers (the medium and little carnivores), primary consumers (the large wild and domestic herbivores, like antelopes, buffaloes, gazelles, elephants, deers, roe-deers, wild boars, and the domestic she-buffaloes, cows, sheep, goats, etc.), humans and decomposers.

And as they maintain the functional structure of the ecosystem, they are sustainable human societies.

He made his main field researches in India, Portugal and Niger, among other countries, like Spain, France, Burkina Faso or South Africa, sometimes with very short money, or even any money for more than three times.

He was pioneer in this research field, and has been also a pioneer on the detailed study of the cultures of the Gurjar (Gujjar) Hindu tribe cattle herders in India, and on the Gourmantché tribe, of bow and poisoned arrows' hunters, collecting, agriculturalists and herders in South-West Niger (East Gourma), (and in Burkina Faso).

He already made two Thesis, published eight scientific books (in France, USA, Spain, Portugal, Brazil and India), and many scientific articles and texts.

He is also a literature writer, having published two novels and five books of poetry in Portugal.

Presently he lives in Porto, Portugal, Iberia, European Union, but during large periods of his life he travelled, lived or worked in many countries of four continents, from the USA till Burma (Myanmar), and from Polar regions till the largest Sahara Desert, always in close contact with the local human populations and ecosystems.

Preface

to "Coexistence among Human Societies and Ecosystems. The Geopolitical Elimination of the Common Lands and its Effects on Our Present Global Condition. From Nature to the Artificial Simulacrum World", from João Pedro Galhano Alves.

Farid Benhammou,
Environmental Geographer (France)

Those who know Pédro (for Spanish and French speakers) or João Pedro (for Portuguese speakers) know that he is a free, rich and wandering spirit. He was very early challenged by Claude Levi-Strauss' famous phrase: "I hate travels and explorers".

The founding author of contemporary anthropology said in this that there was no place for exoticism and an overhanging Western-centric approach. If Pedro loved traveling and explore, it was precisely to build bridges between European populations - the mainly Portuguese rural society he knows well, and urban techno-industrial societies - and societies from so-called Southern countries: Sariska Valley in India, with the Gurjar tribe and tigers, and the W region in Niger with the Gourmantché tribe and lions, one of the last peoples still hunting with bow and arrows.

Each time, he apprehends these societies, these cultures with the same humility and openness that led him to speak several languages in order to enter into affinity with his interlocutors who become companions of life. He aspires to a total anthropology seeking common features in the relationships of these human societies to their environment to better criticize the contemporary mechanisms of destruction of life and biotopes.

Doctor. João Pedro Galhano Alves delivers here a classic and original reflection on the state of our societies and environments in their close interrelationships. Although he has a fairly classical vision of ecosystems, his fieldwork – mainly in India, Portugal and Niger – and his readings, have led him to address the vital links that link societies to their environment in the context of a profitable co-evolution.

This is what French geographer Christophe Grenier calls geodiversity, which is articulated with the concept of ecological unconscious developed by our author. This ecological unconscious is or has been the characteristic of humanity and several societies - including the dominant Western society - have tended to bury or even "acculturate" this deep link between humans, the living in the broad sense (non-human animals, plants, bacteria, soils) and the physical substrate (air, minerals, water) that have helped us for millennia to live on Earth and to establish the most sustainable lifestyles and interrelations possible with the environments.

But it's not just ecosystems that are at risk. Societies with the most sustainable communal lifestyles have been as much the victims as natural environments degraded by short-term capitalist development with unsustainable mining logics, or by "Wilderness policies".

J.P. Galhano Alves will try to dissect these processes in his own way, in a way that is both simple and erudite. Transversality is its watchword. The political dimensions are very present, this is a political anthropology of nature conservation work.

Nature where the human is considered as an integral and not an external part of it, as Philippe Descola has so well popularized. In this, it is also geopolitics of conservation, in the sense that we find Gaya – the Earth – in the very etymology of geopolitics.

If references may seem absurd, this Rococo and Classic work has the merit of being in an accessible language and leaves open reflections to use the human and social sciences to advance the protection of life and our environment in the broad sense.

Farid Benhammou, environmental geographer, Laboratoire Ruralités (University of Poitiers, France). Doctor of Agro Paris Tech (France), professor of geography and geopolitics in preparatory classes at the Camille Guérin high school in Poitiers (France).

Preface

to "Coexistence among Human Societies and Ecosystems. The Geopolitical Elimination of the Common Lands and its Effects on Our Present Global Condition. From Nature to the Artificial Simulacrum World", from João Pedro Galhano Alves.

Soumaïla Mordia Wali
Guide and Research Assistant (Niger)

The research missions from the Doctor of Anthropology, João Pedro GALHANO ALVES, in the region of the W National Park of Niger (Niger, West Africa), began in 2001, till 2012.

Today, his deep researches on the local traditional societies and their coexistence with lions and large fauna, in a wild and humanized ecosystem of Total Biodiversity, are essential.

Since the beginning of our collaboration, as a Guide but also as Research Assistant, I was immediately very impressed by his way of working in the field.

We walked in the savannah may days, sometimes by night.

We never saw before a researcher that may live in a little village, isolated in the savannah, during long periods, and during his 12 years of Post-Doctorates in Anthropology an Ethnobiology.

He was the first scientific researcher that sleeps and lived in a village of the W of Niger region, in this case, our little village of Moli Haoussa(-Gourma). His researches in the region have a great importance. They are the first, and till now unique, long-term researches. And they are pioneer in the scientific field.

The results of these researches had been totally published in a book which title is: “Anthropologie et Ecosystèmes au Niger. Humains, lions et esprits de la forêt dans la culture gourmantché“ (L’Harmattan, Paris, France, 2012).

The observations and analyses of Doctor J.P. Galhano Alves, on the traditional practices, culture and rituals of the region, on the Goumantché Tribe, and on the Ethnobiology of the lion and biodiversity, allow him to perceive and create new concepts and rules that must allow our deciders to better take conscience of the importance of Nature, and of the material and immaterial cultural richness of the studied peoples.

The traditional societies that live in perfect harmony with their natural and humanised ecosystems are models to other cases. To live for a long time, Humanity must stop his marginalisation of Nature and of the traditional societies which still know how to live in “Total Biodiversity” or “High Biodiversity”.

Acknowledgements

This book is dedicated to the memory of late Professor Pierre Coulomb (France, 1937–1995), who taught me the structural and strategic importance of land use and property systems, during the years when I was his disciple and he has been my Co-Director of Research in DSPU and Master of Science of High Studies, between 1989 and 1995 (Centre International de Hautes Etudes Agronomiques Méditerranéennes / Institut Agronomique Méditerranéen de Montpellier, France ; Adana University, Turkey). In this work I try, in part, to developpe his thinking.

Learning from Doctor Armando Salgado Rodrigues (Porto, Portugal; Cleveland, Ohio, USA) in the 1970s and 1980s made me conscious of both the complexity of politics and human behavior.

Professor José Luis Salinas was my Research Director in DSPU and Master of Science of High Studies, between 1993 and 1995, and latter he helped me in the making of the conceptual analyses of this book. Its thanks to him, and to my Co-Directors of Research, Professor Pierre Coulomb and Doctor Alain Bourbouze, that I made my multidisciplinary pioneer researches about humans, tigers and biodiversity in India, and about the Hindu tribe Gurjar (Centre International de Hautes Etudes Agronomiques Méditerranéennes / Institut Agronomique Méditerranéen de Montpellier, Montpellier, France).

I'll never forget the teachings and support of the Research Director of my Doctorate in Anthropology, Professor Jean-Luc Bonniol (Laboratoire d'Écologie Humaine et d'Anthropologie - Centre National de Recherche Scientifique - CNRS, Université d'Aix-

Marseille III, Aix-en-Provence, France). It was under his direction that I did a new part of my researches on humans and tigers in India, and my researches on humans, wolves and biodiversity in Portugal, Europe, and in the World (I was pioneer on a multidisplinary and detailed approach of this subject).

Professors Serge Bahuchet (Laboratoire d'Ethnobiologie, Muséum National d'Histoire Naturelle, CNRS, Paris, France) and Artur Cristóvão (Departamento de Economia, Sociologia e Gestão, Universidade de Trás-os-Montes e Alto Douro, Vila Real, Portugal) gave me support and directed my first steps of the writing of this book, in 2003, and they directed my researches during my first three years of my Post-Doctorates (2000-2004).

I am also very thankful to the Professors Amélia Frazão Moreira (Departamento de Antropologia, Universidade Nova de Lisboa, Portugal), and Danièle Vazeilles (Département d'Ethnologie, IRSA, Université Paul Valéry - Université de Montpellier III, France), who directed and supported my research activity during the height last years of my Post-Doctorates (2004-2012). Professor Danièle Vazeilles supported scientifically the writing of this book, as well as other publications in that period.

It is thanks to these late Research Directors that I made my studies on humans, lions and biodiversity in Niger. A detailed multidisciplinary work that was also pioneer at an African and international levels, on the ethnobiology of lion, and on the multidisciplinary description of the culture of Gourmantché tribe.

Dialogues with Doctor Hassan Kamil, researcher in Anthropology (Montpellier, France), and with Mr. António Maria Mendes Melo (Comissão de Coordenação e Desenvolvimento da Região Norte, Porto, Portugal), were significant in the exchange of ideas and data.

The data of field research works were collected in India, Portugal, Niger and other countries, thanks to the support of the villages' inhabitants and of the local authorities and researchers. In India, in the Sariska Tiger Reserve (Rajasthan) I was a guest of the family of Mr. Baxi Gurjar and Mr. Um Rao Gurjar, in Haripura village. And I had as translator and key informer Mr. Pool Chand Bunker.

In Niger, in the region of the W of (the river) Niger, I was a guest in the village of Moli Haoussa(-Gourma) at the family of the Gourmantché Chief, Mr. Talimbaré Kondjoua, from the Clan of the Lion, and at the family of the Haoussa Chief, Mr. Abdou Noma. And I had as translator and key informer Mr. Soumaïla Mordia Wali, a young polyglot, cultivated and informed Gourmantché, a very intelligent man, from the Gourmantché Clan of the Crocodile.

In Portugal, in the Montesinho Natural Park, in the village of Varge, I hired a room at the family of Mr. José Manuel Gonçalves, who gave me other logistic facilities. And I had as key informer Mr. Vitorino Lourenço. And, in August 1997, my mother, Dr. Maria José Couto Galhano Alves, and my Spanish girl-friend Doctor María Blanco Fonseca, joined me in Varge village, helping me in logistic needs, as a car to reach several villages of the region, Portuguese or Spanish, in that trans-frontier territory.

In the main towns, in New Delhi, India, I have been adopted like a blood brother by the family of Mrs. Sajid Bai Nizami and Taj Mohamed Nizami, in Adhchini Village area. And in Niamey, Niger, I was a guest of Mr. Djibrilla Moussa' family, in the Quartier Faisal, and of the family of my Wife and of our Son, Her Highness the Peul Princess of Say (Niger), Madam Sahadatou Abdoulaye Niandou, and our Infant, David Ismael Niandou Galhano Alves.

In India I had scientific support from Doctor Anil Agarwal (Centre for Science and Environment, New Delhi), since 1992, and from Doctor Vasumati Shankara (Indian Institute of Public Administration, New Delhi), since 1994. I also met latter in Paris, France, Doctor Anil Agarwal, when he had been taken in charge by French State, to treat a cancer, that was fatal. He has been my "Guru" in the definition of research topics and choice of regions to make the fieldwork. He led me to the study of the Ethnobiology of the Tiger in India, and the Ethnobiology of Lion in Africa. In Portugal I learned a lot from the wolf and ecology specialist Mr. Luís Moreira (Montesinho Natural Park): And in Niger I had the institutional and scientific support from the Colonel, Member of the Honor Legion of Niger, Dr. Ali Harouna, Director of Fauna of the Niger Government, among many other people.

Without these supports it would be impossible to make the field research works, and this also because my French and latter Portuguese scientific research grants weren't high enough to make them, far from that.

A scientific research grant of DSPU and Master of Science of High Studies, of two years (1993-1995), from the Centre International de Hautes Etudes Agronomiques Méditerranéennes / Institut Agronomique Méditerranéen de Montpellier (Paris and Montpellier, France / OCDE), allowed me to start my research scientific field.

Research grants from the Fundação para a Ciência e Tecnologia, Ministério da Ciência, Tecnologia e Ensino Superior (Lisbon, Portugal) supported the making of my researches during five years of Doctorate (1995-2000) and twelve years of Post-Doctorates (2000-2012).

The scientific and institutional support from Doctor Fernando Palacios Arribas (Departamento de Biodiversidad y Biología Evolutiva, Museo Nacional de Ciencias Naturales - Consejo Superior de Investigaciones Científicas, Madrid, Spain) was essential during my twelve years of Post-Doctorates (2000-2012), but also before, during my Doctorate (1995-2000). He has been a teacher and a master for me, about wolves, its ecology and its situation in Spain and in the World. And, also, on the technics and policies of large fauna survival, conservation and restoration.

Thanks to this Spanish senior-researcher, in 2006 I was invited by the Direction of the National Museum of Natural Sciences, of the Superior Council of Scientific Researches (MNCN-CSIC, Madrid, Spain), to make a large exhibition retrospective of my scientific career, of 900 m2, during twelve months (2010-2011). With my collections of more than four hundred fifty ethnographic and ethnobiological objects that I brought from the villages and cities of Niger, India, Portugal and other countries of Asia, Europe and Africa, a selection of my photographic collection, and descriptive texts of the realities of the research fields, and the formulated analyses and concepts. It was mostly by this exhibition that the Spanish Government participated in the International Year of Biologic Diversity of the United Nations 2010.

In 2017 I gave my collections to the Museu de História Natural e da Ciência da Universidade do Porto (Porto, Portugal) for them to become public.

Professor Maria Almeida (Faculdade de Letras, Universidade do Porto, Portugal) made the revision of the first English version of this book (Galhano Alves, 2009).

I am also thankful to Doctor Farid Benhammou, for his Prefaces to the French and this second edition in English.

Written by João Pedro Galhano Alves, in Madrid (Spain), Montpellier (France) and Porto (Portugal), between 2003 and 2008.

This perfectionated second English language edition was revised, increased and actualized by the author in 2023, in Porto, Portugal, European Union, just after publishing the French version of the book, in February month, in Paris, France (Galhano Alves, 2023).

Introduction

The individual, private, and collectivist appropriation of land, territory, and natural resources is not a general rule of human cultures. On the contrary, throughout the history of the human species, communitarian land use systems have been the most widespread. These systems are based on the natural right of each individual to use land and natural resources in order to survive and live. Land and resource use may be individual, family, or collective, but land is a common space. Even in these systems, however, it has been always accepted that individuals or family units use some land as their own for habitat, vegetable gardens, or agricultural fields.

From an ecological point of view, these systems have several advantages. Most territory has no fences, allowing free movement of wildlife and people; resources are used principally in an extensive way; and different land uses tend to be adapted to micro-ecologic features of each territory's portion. This does not mean that, in many cases, human groups don't erode or destroy common ecosystems. But the general tendency is toward an adaptation to the natural habitat of the ecosystem. In fact, presently high biodiversity ecosystems are mostly located in areas where communitarian land use systems still exist, as is the case in tiger territories in India, wolf ones in Portugal, and lion ones in Niger.

From a social point of view also, those systems have several advantages. Each individual, family group, or the whole community may exist by themselves, and does not depend on external factors to achieve survival. Food, water, fuel, and materials for building and tools may be freely collected or produced from the landscape, which allows a large degree of food, energy, and habitat autonomy for each individual. Harder tasks are shared collectively, as well as common infrastructures. This does not mean that such human groups tend to live in an isolated way; but their autonomy is ensured.

A deep change in systems of land use can be traced to ancient Rome, when the slavery *latifundia* system evolved from former informal individual land appropriations, until the institution, in 111 BC, of a new legal concept: private land property (*lex Thoria*).

Even so, most European territories remained common until the beginning of the Industrial Revolution. First in England, and later in France (where the modern concept of privately owned land property was invented and defined by jurist Pothier in the triptych *Usus, Abusus, Fructus*), then spread globally by colonial expansion, this method of social appropriation of land preceded, everywhere, industrialization and the formation of mass production and consumption societies. The reason for this was clearly expressed in 1793 by French conventioneer Delacroix, who declared, "If we give the land to the people, we will not have a labour force" (for industry, agriculture and armies). Progressive elimination of communitarian land use has been a strategic way of depriving masses of people from free access to survival resources and preventing them from cultivating land, grazing cattle, hunting, or collecting food, fuel, and materials in the natural landscape. In the Leninist state, collectivist property achieved the same goals in a similar way, on the basis of theories by David Ricardo and Karl Marx (Marx, 1883).

Both systems caused the largest mass migrations in human history, as new proletarians were forced to migrate from the countryside to the growing new cities, which soon evolved into the modern megalopolis. This change also implied an intensive exploitation of natural resources to maintain huge urban populations and industrial growth. The strategy was aimed at building up techno-industrial mass production and consumption societies; since the eighteenth century, this type of progress has been valued as a positive will for humankind.

As the masses were deprived of free access to vital resources, they became dependent on the diptych work (i.e., work as an abstract activity independent from personal need or will) and consumption in order to survive, fuelling by such dependence industrial production and consumption, and, so, capital growth. Also, by this process, money became the universal abstract merchandise upon which most people became dependent.

But such dependence does not explain by itself the tendency toward growing mass consumption in such societies. Mass dependence, production, and consumption may be linked, but the tendency toward growing mass consumption is linked with more complex factors. The human attachment behavior system, which is common to many other species, has been deprived of its natural objectives, which are mostly living beings, natural landscapes, and other human beings, which ensure survival and homeostasis of the attachment behavior system. As a consequence, boredom becomes massive. Attachment behavior tends to create links with substitute objects in urban minimal biodiversity environments, but these are usually artificial and inert objects, images, and sounds. This substitution becomes a vicious spiral, because in such environments, natural attachment behavior can't achieve its objectives, which fuels overconsumption of objects, images, and sounds. Moreover, competition for survival in such social structures corrupts a large part of human intra-species[1] attachment possibilities. In this way dependence, work, money, consumption, competition, and industrial and financial capital growth have become a total social fact (in anthropological terminology), which is a total social reality that tends to dominate all spheres of human life. In addition, mass dependency favors a growing mass infantilism, and so favors manipulation and political (local or global) totalitarian systems, even under parliamentary democratic forms of government which respect basic civil rights.

For the same reasons, massive exploitation of nature is an intrinsic requirement of such systems, to fuel their ever-growing intrinsic needs. Furthermore, use of land and resources is dependent on socioeconomic and mass production factors, instead of being adapted to each ecosystem's features and carrying capacity.

Present ecologic and socioeconomic disasters point to a global need for change in social production and consumption systems. But such changes cannot be achieved, most probably, without a change in land and resource appropriation and use systems. Present political

1. Among members of the same species.

movements of urban or peasant groups are oriented for individual, state, or collectivist appropriation of land, maintaining the above-described vicious spiral. On the other hand, the fact of global human overpopulation should curb possible attempts to restore communitarian systems, as a massive migration to natural or agrarian landscapes could cause a faster ecological disaster than the one presently on course.

In this book these processes are explained and analyzed, in order to show how the human species evolved to its present condition.

Keywords

Land use systems; common lands; land property; industrial civilization; ecology; human evolution; rural and ecological policies

I

"Even the wild beasts in the jungle have their dens and caves where they can protect themselves, but the men who fight and die for Italy do not have anything but the air and the light. Deprived of roof, they go wandering with their wives and sons. Commanders cheat the soldiers when in the battlefields they incite them to fight to defend their tombs and homes from the enemies; they lie, because a majority of Romans have neither paternal altar nor ancestors' tomb. They only have the name of world masters, but they must die for others' luxury without being able to call theirs a piece of land." —Tiberius Graco speech (Rome, 134 BC), in Plutarch, *Tiberius Graco, IX*)

"We will see on Earth, creatures which will kill each one without rest. Their wickedness will not have a limit; their violence will destroy the globe's big forests; and even after being full, they will not stop for that their desire of wide spreading carnage, tribulations and exile among all creatures. There will be nothing left on earth, nor under the waters, that will not be persecuted and exterminated, and what is in one country will be deported to the other." —Leonardo Da Vinci (Italy and France, fifteenth and sixteenth centuries)—*Prophecies*

"Yahweh God took the man and settled him in the Garden of Eden to cultivate and take care of it."—The Old Testament, Genesis 2:15

Professor Pierre Coulomb[1] began always his agricultural policies chair dissertation on land property systems with a clear sentence: "Land property is an abstract concept, as we may say that it is neither natural nor logical that someone says that a part of Planet Earth belongs to him."

1. Pierre Coulomb (1937–1995), Professor and researcher on agricultural policies in Paris and Montpellier (France).

Many economic policies of the nineteenth and twentieth centuries are based on wrong interpretations of the evolutionary mechanisms of natural selection, stating that competition, and the consequent imposition of the strongest over the weakest, shall bring social abundance and progress for all.[1] Also, both in liberal capitalist and in Leninist theories, domination and intensive exploitation of nature by human work are the way to reach those social goals.

1. Very differently, Darwin pointed out that "all organized beings try to multiply themselves in a geometric progression; each one of them, in some periods of its life, during some seasons of the year, during each generation, or in some intervals, must fight for existence and is exposed to big destruction. But…war is not incessant in nature…and the ones who survive and multiply themselves are the vigorous, healthy and happy ones" (Darwin, 1859).

II

Living Species and Primate Territorial Behavior; Ecosystems Network

Scientific ecology shows that nature works more by synergic systems than by competition-based systems. Living systems are networks of huge complexity, in which each species and living being has complementary and interdependent functions. In what concerns territorial behavior in particular, we know that even highly territorial animals, such as tigers, wolves, and lions, have variable territory representations. Not only does the territory representation change in space and time, but shifts in the animal's attitude toward intruders or passengers of the same or other species may also vary as a function of synergy, association, attachment, alliance, mutualism, symbiosis, interference, opportunism, competition, parasitism, predation, or indifference factors that may even be imponderable.

Of course, no animal or living being can have a territorial behavior oriented toward total exclusion; a lonely animal without links or vital resources cannot exist, and fixation on that kind of behavior would be energetically unsustainable. A single glimpse of nature provides enough evidence to understand this behavior: Animals and plants of all kinds live, move, and develop their activities in the same area, most of the time in a peaceful way, punctuated by conflictive, ritual-like symbolic confrontations, deadly predatory moments, or even, quite rarely, violent fights.

In very social species, such as primates, this common relationship with space is even more evident. Group association brings to each individual higher protection against predators and weather conditions. It also ensures survival to very young, very old, or sick individuals through attachment and solidarity links. It increases the group's capabilities to find vital resources, and makes possible synergies among each other's skills. Techniques and knowledge are shared in the group, and are developed through time and from generation to generation. For instance, we know that in rhesus macaque societies, each individual deserves its own vital space, which does not have a fixed radius around its body,[1] nor is it exclusive of intrusion or contact with companions. But the whole space and territory is shared and used by group members and other local species as a common land, without purpose of neither abstract or active appropriation. Space and resources are managed according to strategies for safety and well being. These strategies are shaped individually, within the group, and even among members of different species.

1. My observations in Sariska Tiger Reserve (Rajasthan, India, 1985, 1992, 1994, 1996, 2012) indicate that this radius may reach one to two meters for dominant males, and less for other individuals - although other younger or older macaques are always near the bigger males. Concerning primate groups' territorial behavior, it varies as a function of species and ecosystem carrying capacity. Some are very territorial (Rowell, 1967), but total territorial behavior does not exist.

III

Hominid and Human Territorial Behavior; Communitarian Land Use Systems; Total or High Biodiversity; Low or Minimal Biodiversity; Restoration of Biodiversity; Discussion of the "Wilderness Policies"

"They will be in gardens...near rivers, in a true abode."—The Koran, Chapter LIV, *Conclusion*

Anthropology and history show that, as it is logical to expect, hominid and primordial human societies had space and territory representations and group resource management systems similar to those of other primates and social mammals. Those systems, usually called *communitarian*, have been universal in all human societies and civilizations until recent historical times[1]. Normally, each human group considers as its homeland or group territory the area in which the group develops its activities—where its members gather, hunt, grow crops, graze cattle, settle their villages and their technological structures, and spend most of their social and individual lives. Usually for sedentary people, the radius of this territory is directly proportional

1 "While all the History of humanity divided in classes (slavery, feudalism, capitalism) has few more than five millenniums, the communitarian regime (…) existed during hundreds of thousands of years" (Diakov & Kovalev, 1973).

to the distance a man can walk away and return to the settlement in one day. In many rural communities, the core zone of the territory is about two to seven kilometers in radius, the distance reached by cattle herds each day. Hunting-gathering and nomadic agriculture or nomadic grazing societies may use much larger areas through time; some may encompass thousands of square kilometers (like in dry and desert areas) - although, in each period, the core zone is not larger than two to seven kilometers in radius. Normally, neighboring communities may share the space and resources of all or most of the territory, but each community uses primarily the resources in its immediate area. Several communities may also use the same space for different but complementary purposes (e.g., the same space may be shared among many distinct agricultural, grazing, hunting-gathering, and fishing groups coexisting in the same territory).

Conflicts may occur if one or several individuals misuse their natural or traditional rights of resource use. In these cases, communitarian informal or formal local institutions may act to repair the faults or punish the guilty parties. Informal or formal rules may also exist for these cases. In several "primitive" societies, war has been reported to occur more for cultural or sexual reasons, or for reasons of honor, than for resource spoliation or human exploitation goals (Descola, 1986). Micro or large groups might also make war for reasons of expansion or pillage, because they destroyed vital resources within their own territories or because they have a tendency toward domination or accumulation. Nevertheless, and more commonly, human groups and societies create cooperation and associative links among one another, that increase their mutual exchanges of all kinds, for development and security. In general, and throughout human history, among members of a stable community, among neighboring villages or different nations, active peace is the rule, while conflict and war are the exception.

In general, in communitarian land use systems, the territory is indivisible, which means no one can declare that one part of it belongs exclusively to him forever. Also, the territory is not alienable, which means it cannot be sold or given away to anyone. Those rights are logical consequences of one concept: Land and territory do not belong to anybody.

In most civilizations, this has a larger sense, which transcends the human dimension, because in their cultural representations the world is just the common living place of all living beings. This concept was well expressed in 1854 by Duwamish tribe Chief Noah Seattle when he answered a colonial army officer, sent by U.S.A. government to buy the land where his people used to live, that he could not sell it, because it did not belong to him, but to all kinds of beings that lived there (Seattle, 1854).

Indivisibility and inalienability of land have several important implications for space and resource management, use, accessibility, and social distribution.

The concept that territory is considered as a single unit and stays so in time allows human communities to manage the territory as a whole, comprising different but complementary natural and humanized biotopes. If the community's interventions are rational, precaution-oriented, and sustainable, this strategy may lead to an optimization of natural and human productivity and prevent the erosion of resources.

Usually in communitarian land use systems, space and resources are used simultaneously on an individual, family, or collective basis. Individuals and family units have almost total freedom to circulate throughout most of the territory, except in privacy zones, such as other individual or family houses, or in productive structures, such as vegetable gardens, orchards, or handicraft and manufacturing structures. Individuals and family units also have free access to all kinds of vital resources, such as settling space, tools and materials for building, crafting, and manufacturing, minerals, water, game, fish, wild vegetables, firewood, pastures, agricultural land plots, and so forth. This is in accordance with the natural right of each human or living being to use the earth and its natural resources in order to ensure his autonomy, his survival, and his living conditions. It also sets an equitable basis for the social distribution of resources according to the needs and the will of each individual, family, or community.

As well, other structures and productive activities (e.g., the village's roads and trails, fountains, irrigation structures, mills, etc.) are collective in these systems. They are made, shared, utilized, and maintained by the whole community.

Another important trait of these systems is that no member of the community can deliberately destroy, spoil, or monopolize a particular resource, nor claim an oversized portion of territory that might be considered valuable for the other members of the group. This means that no one has the right to abuse his freedom to use those resources and territory. Usually, informal or formal decisions and rules prevent those situations. Obviously, those limits depend also upon the capability of each culture to negotiate risky or destructive situations.

In addition, as I mentioned above, these systems develop informal or formal local communitarian institutions, which usually operate according to participative and democratic principles. These institutions are in charge of the major management of the territory and resources; the distribution of territory and resources among individuals and family units; organizing the calendars for collective production and sociocultural activities; decisions concerning planning and regulation of general activities related to land and resources; and relationships and deals with other communities or social groups, even in large political matters.

From an ecological perspective, these land use systems have intrinsic advantages. All kinds of inert substrates, organisms, plants, and animals live and evolve in the open territory. The balance, efficiency, and productivity of all ecosystems depends upon the system's functional structure, visible in trophic chains and in a never-ending network of psycho-physiologic mechanisms and associative, synergic, reproductive, competition, and predatory interactions, among others, which configure matter, energy, and living fluxes.

In normal conditions in the present Quaternary Period, like in former Secondary and Tertiary ones, the functional structure of most humanized ecosystems is fundamentally composed of primary production species (the spontaneous and the agricultural vegetation, which make the photosynthesis), primary consumers (the wild and the domestic herbivores), secondary consumers (the small and the medium carnivores), tertiary consumers (the large carnivores, such as tigers, lions, wolves, jaguars, pumas or bears), human beings, and decomposers. All elements of these trophic chains have essential and complementary roles in the regulation of the ecosystem's balance and productivity. If in one region all those autochthonous species are present in stable and important populations, I say that the ecosystem is in a state of *total biodiversity*. If local human societies proceed in a proper way, they also have important regulatory functions in the ecosystem (Chartiot, 2003; Degeorges & Nochy, und.; Galhano Alves, 1995, 2000, 2002, 2003, 2011, 2012; Torri, 2005). The term "total biodiversity" was first used informally by Valmik Thapar (und.), but was conceptualized and expanded in France by me, and was later used and developed by other researchers.

I must say that presently most of the planet's ecosystems are no longer in total biodiversity. In fact, mostly since the beginning of the nineteenth century, a huge part of the natural vegetation cover has been destroyed or converted to agriculture or monoculture industrial forestry. Many animal species have been exterminated and, by the present rate, about twenty-five percent of the remaining ones may vanish over the next few decades, shaping what is called a Big Extinction. Only two centuries ago, large wild herbivores and carnivores still existed almost everywhere, and humanity lived in close coexistence with them. But since then, the populations of these species have decreased quickly, and are now fragmented and endangered.

At the origin of this process are destructive and erosive human activities, linked to some societies that became historically dominant. This process has ancient roots, and is common to several civilizations, but it became dominant in Europe and accompanied the overseas expansion.

Consequently, most territories are now in a state of *low or minimal biodiversity*, as I called it (Chartiot, 2003; Galhano Alves, 1995, 2000, 2002, 2003, 2011, 2012; Torri, 2005), particularly in productivist agrarian and urban systems in which the remaining species are basically man and a few varieties of domestic vegetables and animals. These systems are fundamentally managed only by one species - man (Homo sapiens *sapiens*, or, Homo sapiens *demens*, as proposed Edgar Morin to the French Academy). The low ecological complexity of these systems makes them unsustainable in the long term. Huge amounts of work and energy are needed for their maintenance. Their high productivity is only apparent. In fact, they are less productive than total or high biodiversity humanized ecosystems, in which balance and productivity are intrinsically high without the need for such large amounts of work and energy (Galhano Alves, 2000, 2002, 2003).

This means that, in effective and sustainable humanized ecosystems, wild and domestic animals of several species, including large herbivores and carnivores, live, move, and evolve in the territory, sharing it with human societies. Large wild and domestic herbivores need substantial natural vegetation, forest, and scrub-covered areas to graze. The territories of large carnivores are even wider, as they are at the top of trophic chains. For instance, the hunting territory of one single tiger in northern India is about fifty square kilometers, and a wolf pack needs an average of seventy-five square kilometers in Mediterranean regions. Obviously, animal populations must be continuous in space to ensure their survival, so these numbers have little sense for long-term conservation. Species distribution areas used to be of continental or subcontinental size.

At this point we can conceptualize the advantages and the potential of communitarian land use systems for integrated and sustainable territory management. Indivisibility of most territory allows freedom of movement for all kinds of species. In these systems, enclosures and fences are rare, except in individual or family fields, villages, and quarters. A suitable use of the territory permits the preservation and even improvement of different biotopes and large significant areas of natural and semi-natural vegetation, forests, woods, and pastures, which are the pillars of the whole ecosystem's functional structure, by their photosynthesis action. Management of natural resources as a common patrimony is a suitable basis to prevent abusive and destructive uses of resources, and facilitates balanced ecosystems. Even in private use areas, such as agricultural fields, communitarian regulatory institutions may have a balancing role.

Because each of the multiple local entities (i.e., individual, family, and collective) has access to the different biotopes and resources, it may be possible to balance the intensity of usage for each resource. Also, as I mentioned above, this practice ensures equitable and diverse access to each resource for each member of the local society, which increases social sustainability. Simultaneously, if a human society maintains high or total biodiversity in its territory, each biotope and the whole ecosystem are regulated and used by a huge number of other small and large living species. This biodiversity improves and may maximize ecologic sustainability, balance, and productivity. It also increases and diversifies the resources for humans and other species.

Until recent times, and mostly until the industrial era, communitarian type of territory representation, use, and management systems were widely common in all continents, human cultures, and civilizations. We may say that these communitarian systems were the natural and universal manner of humankind and society to represent, use, and link themselves with the space, the ecosystem, and its resources. Therefore, very probably communitarian land use may also correspond to an adaptation structure that, since the most ancestral origins of the species, helps human groups and societies to survive and to improve their living conditions. And this is so because it is apt to optimize intra-species[1] and inter-species[2] alliance, association, and synergy.

Throughout history, as in different cultures, communitarian systems have taken several forms. For instance, I have been doing research in northern India among human societies located within the Sariska Tiger Reserve region (Rajasthan). Most inhabitants of this region are from Gurjar (*Gujjar*) tribe, cattle-raising people who graze their she-buffaloes, cows, and goats' herds in forest pastures, for the production of milk. As Hindus, they do not eat meat and are milk-vegetarians. Thus, they do not hunt. They have a close coexistence with tigers, other large carnivores, and large wild herbivores. Their cultural representations of nature and man's place in nature are of the *systemic type*, as I called them. This means they represent vegetation, wild and domestic herbivores, carnivores, and humans as complementary and interdependent elements of the ecosystem, a kind of cultural representation similar to the modern scientific ecological one. Their grazing, gathering, and other production systems are well integrated with the environment, in order to create *synergies* with each species or element within the environment. Consequently, they have been able to conserve total biodiversity over centuries (Galhano Alves, 1995, 1999, 2000, 2002; Galhano Alves & Garcia.Perea, 1998).

1. Among members of the same species.
2. Among members of diferent species.

However, in 2004, an illegal poaching and trade international organization killed all Sariska tigers to sell their body parts in international markets. Tigers vanished in 2004 by factors alien to local cultures, as I predicted formerly in my thesis, articles and speeches (Galhano Alves, 1995, 1999, 2002; Galhano Alves & Garcia-Perea, 1998).

In 2006, Dr. Raghuvir Shekhawat, Field Director of Sariska Tiger Reserve, imported six tigers from Ranthambore Protected Area, more than 500 Km away (2 males and four females). This Forest Officer is a very competent, cultivated and endured environment conservationist. This was the first, and till now unique, reintroduction of tigers in the World. Even with the presence of humans, as local societies are respectful of the environment, tigers multiplied, and are now (in 2023) of 36 in this humanized ecosystem again in state of total biodiversity. A record, taking in account that in 1994 there were 22 tigers, the average medium in the past.

Unfortunately, Dr. Raghuvir Shekhawat and the India Government' Project Tiger officers consider that the little local human populations must be put out of the Reserve, in poorest lands, with a low monetary compensation. This is caused by the Anglo-Saxonist "*Wilderness Policies*", mostly from the USA, which consider that human presence is incompatible with wildlife conservation. Even if the local ecosystems are well conservated, in total biodiversity, also thanks to the behavior and land use systems of the local human populations and cultures, and this for millenniums of years.

This is a tradition since the beginning of the first National Park in the World, the Yellowstone National Park, in the USA, in 1872. The region, rich in megafauna, including Grizzly bears, wolves, cougars, bison, elk and antelopes, was inhabited by humans since 11 000 years ago, by the obsidian Clovis culture. In 1885 a colonial exploratory mission encountered there this macrofauna, large forests, rivers, and the human inhabitants of the region, from the Native American Tribes Perce, Crow and Shoshone. In spite of the synergic integration of the local cultures with the environment, kept in a state of total biodiversity by local societies, they were expulsed from the National Park area, of almost 9 000 Sq.Km. Lead by a thinking in the Act of Dedication of the Park creation, that says that "...is hereby reserved and withdrawn from settlement , occupancy, or sale under the laws of the United States...

and all persons who shall locate, or settle upon, or occupy … shall be considered trespassers and remove there from…”.

Concerning again Sariska Tiger Reserve, in 2012 I met again Mr. Um Rao Gurjar, a former inhabitant of Haripura village, in which house I lived in 1994 and 1996, in the center of the Tiger Reserve. He accepted the money to leave the village and the region with his family. With that money he couldn’t buy more than one hectare of poor land, with limited irrigation, and the money wasn’t also enough to build a house. His family, with children, was living under an improvised tent, and the monsoon was to came. The she-buffaloes didn’t have good pasture. Mr. Um Rao Gurjar never made agriculture, only jungle grazing, so his performances in his field would be low. The “translocation” (migration) of this Gurjar tribe family, descendent from Mr. Baxi Gurjar, ended in a tragedy

In my opinion the “*Wilderness Policies*” are wrong, and they are guilty by making the ethnocide of the local cultures, and bring poverty to the people. At the same time, the local ecosystems, which included human, cattle and little agriculture activities, tend to became poorest[1] (Galhano Alves, 1995, 2000, 2002, 2003).

The “Wilderness Policies” had been created by the western culture, thinking that all kind of societies and cultures are inapt to conserve Nature, like it-self is. This is a projection of its defaults on all other human cultures and natural resource use systems. And this is a wrong thinking and its resulting actions in the fields are also wrong.

On the contrary, these local peoples have the ecological knowledge to conserve their environments in a state of total or high biodiversity, and this for millenniums till the present. And this knowledge may be a reference to other peoples, to live in total biodiversity if their ecosystems are restored, as they must be.

Also, eradicating local rural traditional societies, the territory gets opened for illegal and commercial poaching, as the inhabitants, and mostly the herders or the gather-hunters, are the “eyes of the wild”, being testimonies of poachers’ activities, what dissuades the poachers[2].

1. In 1994 I calculated that the domestic cattle was a minority but significant part of tigers’ food, in Sariska Tiger Reserve (Rajasthan, India) (Galhano Alves, 1995, 2002).
2. This was comprehended by Dr. Raghuvir Shekhawat, Field Director of Sariska Tiger Reserve (Rajasthan, India), who told me in 2012 that he gave a mobile phone to

Also, we must not speak anymore about conservation only in some relatively little areas, like the present protected zones, as this policy does not ensure survival of the wild species for the future. Fauna populations are relatively little and are isolated ones from the others, with their survival in risk. Instead, we should speak about *restoration of biodiversity*, in large areas around the protected zones, till the isolated populations increase in number and distribution areas, till be linked ones to the others. And this implies coexistence with local human societies. That's one of the reasons why it is so important to study the present coexistence between people and wildlife in regions that conserve high or total biodiversity, to understand how their agrarian systems and culture preserved high or total biodiversity through millenniums of years, till the present.

People and conserved or restored ecosystems must be united, and in synergy among humans, large wild carnivores, large wild and domestic herbivores, and the whole environment. As a whole organism. This is the condition both to biodiversity increase, conservation and restoration, and to the human ecodevelopment[1] or sustainable development[2] (French call it *développement durable*, meaning durable development[3]).

In my opinion, the conservation of the remaining wildlife and high biodiversity territories is not ensured for the future, as they are little areas relatively to the whole territories, that are eroded and destroyed[4]. And the wildlife populations are little, fragmentated and isolated. It is so necessary to restore (more than "conserve") the high or total

---

one person in each village of the jungle, with money to call the Forest Officers to denounce poachers or other problems in their area. And poaching of tigers or other wild animals ended.

1. Concept created by the late Doctor Anil Agarwal, in India, in the years 1980's and 1990's.
2. Concept created by Henry Kissinger, in the USA, in the 1990's, adopting a word of Economy ("sustainable growing") to Ecology, avoiding discursive contradiction between the two.
3. Former France President of the Republic Dr. Nicolas Sarkozy mentioned often this concept.
4. In South-Africa, Spain and many other countries, many wildlife reserves are fenced, even with electricity fences, as I could see. They are fenced for that the animals don't scape away, impeaching the re-expansion of wildlife, and they are fenced too for that local native people doesn't goes hunt animals, searching for food or by comercial reasons.

biodiversity in progressively large territories around the present protected areas, allowing the natural vegetation, the large wild and domestic herbivores, and the large carnivores re-expansion, restoring by this manner the biodiversity in territories that will meet each-others.

And keeping the local human populations, giving them education campaigns on ecology and on sustainable development. The re-expansion of natural vegetation may be obtained by reforestation campaigns, or by "setting aside" several areas, conserving enough territory, but not dominant, for agriculture and forestry.

Concerning again Sariska Tiger Reserve, the Gurjar tribe' representation of territory and resources does not have a defined, property-like regime. In practice, all the land, the whole jungle, is used and managed by villagers as a common territory. Somehow, the territory that surrounds each village is considered as "its" territory, but there is not a formal land use system of rules.

Thus, land has neither enclosures nor fences, and all villagers and their cattle herds have free access to the resources on an equal opportunity basis. Ecologic processes and wild fauna movements are also ensured.

Panchayats, the local representative assemblies, composed by elected delegates from several villages, take on decisions for large zones, but within each village there is no formal deciding or regulatory institution. At this level, as Gurjar people explain, "Community decisions are taken together in the village, when weather is cold and men speak around the fire." Individual abuses of resource use are regulated in an informal way or, if they are serious, by more formal rules. For instance, to paraphrase a local farmer, if a person were to kill a sacred wild animal (in principle, all of them are sacred for the Hindus, as they consider that all individual animals have an *Atma* - Soul), "All the people from the village would make a meeting and would punish the guilty one. For example, they would oblige him to pay a fine, or they would oblige him to feed one hundred people in the temple" (Galhano Alves, 1995, 1999, 2000, 2002; Galhano Alves, & Garcia-Perea, R., 1998; Torri, 2005).

Terrasse of a house of she-buffaloes, caws and goats' herders of the Gurjar Hindu tribe, in Haripura village, in the jungle of Sariska Tiger Reserve (Rajasthan, Bharat / India, South Asia). An ecosystem in state of total biodiversity, including tigers - Photo © J.P. Galhano Alves, 1994.

A hunter of the Gourmantché tribe with bow and arrows (with poison) and other weapons, from the Moli Haoussa(-Gourma) village, in the savannah of the W National Park region (East Gurma, Niger, West Africa). An ecosystem in state of total biodiversity, including lions - Photo © J.P. Galhano Alves, 2002.

A herder of sheep in the area of Rio de Onor village, in Montesinho Natural Park (Trás-os-Montes, North-East of Portugal, Iberian Peninsula, Western Europe). An ecosystem in state of high biodiversity, including wolves - Photo © J.P. Galhano Alves, 1997.

In Africa, communitarian land use systems also used to be prevalent over other kinds of land appropriation. For example, between 2000 and 2012 I made researches among human societies from W National Park region (East Gourma), in Niger (West Africa). Local villages are inhabited mostly by Gourmantché tribe people, along with Hausa, Peul, Tuareg, and Bariba[1] people. Family units live mainly on agriculture, cattle-raising, gathering and bow and arrow (poisoned) hunting,. They coexist with lions, elephants, buffaloes, antelopes, and other large African species, in a tree-savannah humanized ecosystem which is in a state of total biodiversity. Their representations of nature are of Gourmantché "animist" type, mixed with other Islamic, Christian, and Tuareg representations, and also with modern scientific ecological representations that are common among local young people. They believe that invisible spiritual beings from Nature regulate both wildlife and human existence, shaping what I call a *parallel-systemic* representation of nature and man's place in nature. The word they use

1. In the village of Moli Haoussa(-Gourma), there was only a Bariba man. This people is becoming extinct in West Africa.

to encompass the whole forest and its spiritual beings is *Fuhaly*, which means both "forest" and "the whole of all beings." This indicates they perceive nature as a whole of connected beings (Galhano Alves, 2007a, 2007b, 2008, 2009b, 2011, 2012).

In these societies, territory and resources are used in a communitarian way. The right to use and reap land and resources is ensured to all individuals and families, but no one can abuse it. Concerning the distribution of field areas, the villagers say, "Each adult more than 18 years old and unmarried has right to 0.25 hectare of agricultural land, as a minimum. If he is married, he has more.[1] It depends on his capacity and will to work. There are unmarried ones that cultivate almost 1 ha, and some married ones that do less than 0.5 ha. Also, there are no conflicts, neither for water nor because of bad private soil managements, nor for other reasons. Normally, each family uses always the same fields…Unless if someone emigrates and gives his field to a friend to use it for free. It may also happen that a field becomes uncultivated and forest grows up there again." To clear and cultivate a new plot of land, each person must ask the village chief for permission. Informal debate about land questions is also made among people. If conflicts linked to field land occur, the villagers have a meeting among some leading family members to resolve it. Normally, this communitarian council comprises the village chief and one "old man" from each ethnic group.

Concerning the forest, even these informal use rules do not exist. The villagers describe this free use system as follows: "For the ones who live in the village the forest is free. But if a foreigner wants to gather wood, grass or to clear and cultivate a plot, must ask for permission to the village chief…It never happened that someone uses the forest in a bad manner, taking too much wood or grass. Nevertheless, if that would happen, measures would be taken against that person" (Galhano Alves, 2007a, 2007b, 2008, 2009b, 2011, 2012).

In America, throughout almost all its precolonial history, territories were used on a communitarian basis, except perhaps during a few and atypical collectivist-like pre-Columbian empires. The same is true among Arctic, Australian, and Polynesian societies.

1. In this region, these areas are the minimum size necessary to sustain the food and energy needs of an adult person and an average number of people who depend on her, such as children and the elderly.

In Europe, communitarian territory and land use systems have been widespread throughout most of its history. For instance, in several Celtic societies, which thrived in Europe and in the Near East for over five centuries until Roman military invasions,[1] many agricultural lands were communitarian. Each year the plots were distributed among inhabitants, and harvests were shared by all. Forests and pastures were also used on a communitarian basis (Sopeña, 2002). In other Celtic tribes, farming land didn't belong to the individual but to the family, although most probably other lands were common (Powell, 1958). Among Germanic cultures land use systems were similar (e.g., in Visigoth societies).

I must mention that these systems have even older origins, because they have been continuous since Paleolithic and Neolithic times. Presently, despite an onslaught of historical vicissitudes, communitarian land use systems remain in several European regions.

For example, in Portugal, traditionally productive lands near villages are divided into plots, which are used separately by family units for vegetable, fruit, green pasture, and cereal production, among other things. However, the majority of the territory is common land (*baldio*), including not only hilly zones, pastures, scrubs, and forests, but also some arable land. Portuguese communitarian territory management and use systems are heterogeneous; they vary according to each region's traditions. Nevertheless, presently among villages in the Montesinho Natural Park region, in the northeast of the country, they hold in common that each inhabitant of all villages has the right to use common space and resources individually, in family units, and collectively. Different types of communitarian councils elected by the whole population, or representing all families, regulate land use, distribute arable plots, sanction tree cut-downs, and organize collective production and cultural activities (Dias, 1984; Rodrigues, 1987; Galhano Alves, 1994b; Ribeiro et al., 2004).

In the Montesinho Natural Park region, in Trás-os-Montes, North-East of Portugal, Iberia, Europe), unlike most of Western Europe, biodiversity remains high. Local human societies coexist

1. Celtic societies prevailed all over Central and Western Europe, and in the Near East, from the fifth century BC until the Roman invasions between the first century BC and the first century AD.

with wolves, wild boar, deer, and roe deer - even if, since the Middle Ages, they have persecuted these species; exterminated bear, lynx, and other species[1]; and destroyed most native forests. Such *conflictive* and *biocidal* relationships with wildlife are linked with (what I call) *not-systemic* representations of nature and of man's place in nature. In Europe, at least since the Middle Ages, man has been considered "superior to all animals," and as Christian Bible states, "his mission is to dominate earth and all creatures."[2] Living beings are depicted as "useful or useless, good or bad," shaping an anthropocentric, dichotomous, and Manichean representation of nature, maladjusted to the mechanisms of real ecosystems. This is reflected also in the agrarian, resource management, and production systems of these cultures. However, if in the Montesinho region high biodiversity remains alive, it is thanks to some atypical and positive local cultural representations of wolf, and to several aspects of its agrarian system. Among these are extensive family agriculture and the lasting (until a few decades ago) of communitarian management and use of territory and resources. Presently, these structures are a favorable base for both wildlife conservation and the enhancement of human living conditions (Galhano Alves, 1994a, 2000, 2002). For example, wolf distribution area is increasing in the North of Portugal. Moreover, in Europe as elsewhere, a majority of those regions where biodiversity remains high are the ones where most of the territory remains communitarian - or did so up until recently.

---

1. Portuguese people did also exterminate several species in the global Empire (from XVth century till the XXth century). Like, for example, the big bird Dodo, in the Mauritius Island, in the Indic Ocean. This bird was declared extinct in 1681 DC, less than one hundred years after the arrival of the Dutch people (since 1598 AD) and, before, the Portuguese one (since 1507 AD).
2. Literally, the Jewish text says in the book of Genesis: "God blessed them, saying to them, 'Be fruitful, multiply, fill the earth and subdue it. Be masters of the fish of the sea, the birds of the sky and all the living creatures that move on earth" (La Sainte Bible, 1966, Gen. 1:28). However, some of its other assertions, which perhaps come from cultural traditions different from those which shaped the former sentence, have a contradictory meaning. For instance, in the same book of Genesis, one can read: "Yahweh God took the man and settled him in the garden of Eden to cultivate and take care of it" (La Sainte Bible, 1966, Gen. 2:15).

IV

History of the Plunder and Destruction of the Common Territories and Resources; Formation of the Capitalist Mass Production and Consumption Industrial Societies; Land Private Property; Progress; Economic Growth; Development; Egalitarianism; Future

"Young man, why do you make so much noise? Your conch woke me up from my sleep. All the human beings in these parts are kind to animals. You seem to be a stranger to this place. You are not considerate towards the inmates of this place. Where do you come from? Who are you? Beyond this spot this forest is impregnable. In kindness I am telling you this, kindness towards a fellow human being. I am sure you will listen to me. Here are some fruits. Eat them. Rest awhile here and go back to where you come from. You cannot go any further than this. I tell you the truth." - Monkey God Hanuman, *Mahabharata*, Chapter 12[1].

The history of the plunder and destruction of common territories and resources is a bloody sequence of violence, terror, massacre,

1. This part of the sacred Hindu book Mahabharata ("The-Great-India") is located in the region of the present Sariska Tiger Reserve (Rajasthan, India), exactly in the site of Pandupol.

swindling and exploitation. It couldn't be any other way, since only through violence and manipulation could a single human, entire nations, and the other living species be deprived of their natural right to feed and warm themselves, and to move freely on Earth.

In Europe, the origin of this process can be traced back to Greek and Roman slavery societies. In early periods of Roman history, most territory was *communal* (*ager publicus*); it belonged to the state, because the Roman community was a city-state (*polis*), and farmers paid taxes to cultivate plots. Probably this communal property tradition evolved from ancestral communitarian land use systems when militarization of the city became dominant. Subsequently, by the fifth century BC, communal property did break down. Rich citizens occupied the best lands and considered those lands to "belong" to them, starting a process of intrinsic primitive capital-land accumulation and exploitation of the poor workforce. Military expansion through the Mediterranean amplified this process; conquered lands and resources were stolen, their inhabitants were made slaves by millions, and a huge mass of subproletariat appeared also among Romans. By the second century BC massive slavery had become a specific Roman system, never seen before in the ancient world. Dispossessed people became a never-ending source of soldiers, who sustained the system by violence.

In 111 BC, Espurio Thorium law (*lex Thoria*) abolished the last restriction to *private ownership of land property*, declaring formerly communal lands as property of the occupiers (an important part of Roman territorial expansion), and deeming as communal the remaining area - whatever survived consecutive occupations.

For about five centuries, intensive land and slave exploitation led to huge capital accumulation. But the simultaneous circumstances of soil and resource erosion (principally in Italy and Sicily), mass rebellions of slaves, the low productivity rate of slavery and enormous *latifundia*, and *democrats'* assumptions that *latifundia* and slavery were somehow unnatural,[1] generated another form of exploitation—

1. A speech of tribune Tiberius Graco in 134 BC, reported by Plutarch, expresses this clearly: "Even wild beasts in the jungle have their dens and caves where they can protect themselves, but the men who fight and die for Italy do not have anything but the air and the light. Deprived of roof, they go wandering with their wives and sons. Commanders cheat the soldiers when in the battlefields incite them to fight to defend their tombs and homes from the enemies, they lie, because a majority of Romans

the renting out of plots of large estates to the people (*colonies*). The colonies increased the production cost-to-profit rates but did not stop the land property concentration. Tenant farmers (*colons*) accumulated debts to landowners, and progressively approached the status of serfdom. During the fourth and fifth centuries AD, imperial edicts deprived *colons* of translocation freedom, transforming them into real serfs. Meanwhile, mass poverty had a fatal effect on handicraft, trade, and military structures. When in the night of 24th August 410 AD Roman slaves opened the doors of the city of Rome to Alaric's Goths army - which became stronger with the support of forty thousand rebelled slaves - the foundations of the feudal society were done (Kovaliov, 1948).

The fact that lions became extinct in Europe during the Roman Empire is symptomatic of the erosion of biodiversity and natural resources caused by the Empire's accumulative character. Greco-Roman culture had several anthropocentric features, depicted, for instance, in the story of Prometheus.[1] However, Roman cultural and religious structures still had strong links with nature; for instance, since in Rome the She-Wolf had a master role in the city's origin, the species was almost sacred. At the fall of the Empire, European ecosystems still had a high biodiversity structure. The main wave of global destruction was yet to come.

Medieval land property structures seem to be a combination of late Roman serfdom and older communal ones, with communitarian systems conserved or re-established by formerly occupied European societies. The whole land use system was under the violent rule and the military, political, and economic domination of the feudal landlords, who took possession of land and people by war.

Moorish and Ottoman regimes, at the edges of Western Europe, may not have altered this situation substantially, because they were mostly based on tax imposition. However, in the Iberian Peninsula,

---

have neither paternal altar nor ancestors' tomb. They only have the name of world masters, but they must die for others' luxury without being able to call theirs a piece of land" (in *Tiberius Graco*, IX). In the following year of 133 BC, Tiberius Graco and three hundred of his democrat partisans were assassinated by the senators in Rome.

1. In Protagoras' version of the Prometheus myth, written by Plato, "Man had his part of the gods' lot," because he received the gods' techniques and arts, but such gifts were given to him to balance his lack of capabilities that had been given to the "beasts that do not speak" (Plato, 399–390 BC).

the Moors had communitarian systems of territory use that could have favored partial re-establishment of autochthonous communitarian structures, improved by early Arab agricultural skills and cultural tolerance.[1]

The rising or imposition of Christianity as a unique religion in its Old Testament form also had severe ecological consequences. In fact, although Jesus' teachings are centered on love, life, and a sort of spiritual wandering-like freedom, Christian churches accentuate the anthropocentric, Manichean, and repressive features of the Old Testament, fitting to servitude and manipulation, both of which helped erase whatever remained of ancestral European "animist" cultures and supported the dominant classes, which then provided for the needs of the clergy. The reaction of Saint Francis of Assisi to this situation had limited results.

Thereafter, a huge persecution of wildlife began, and did not stop until the present. When firing weapons, poison, and machinery use became generalized after the eighteenth century, the rate of species extinction became exponential. But the destruction of biodiversity and habitats was also a consequence of cumulative oversized land and resource exploitation, existing since Roman and even pre-Roman times, crossing the Middle Ages until the present. Despite that, since Antiquity, destructive exploitation has not reached all regions with equal intensity. Hilly, marginal, or nonstrategic lands were used in a less erosive way. There, autochthonous agricultural, grazing, and hunting-gathering semi-autarchic systems, both familiar and communitarian, remained over the centuries. It is mainly in those regions where high or total biodiversity remained alive, not only in Europe but also in the other continents.

Throughout history, other human civilizations, by similar violent methods, developed mass land deprivation systems, slavery, feudal-like societies, huge war structures, military empires, and created massive deforestation, wildlife destruction, and arable soil erosion. This is the case, for example, of Mesopotamian and Chinese civilizations, among others, as well as smaller human groups such as the Easter

1. In Mediterranean Islamic cultures, land property rules include common lands, freely used by tribes, families, and individuals, in addition to general state land property rules and religious institutions (Bourbouse & Rubino, 1992).

Island communities. But evolution of those processes in Europe led to present global status quo.

At least since the Renaissance period (e.g., since fourteenth century), European proto-capitalism was being configured by the development of manufacturing, trade, and finance centers in the cores of towns and along roads; by the transcontinental Venetian trade; and by the consecutive global trading expansion by the seas of the Portuguese and other kingdoms. Business surmounted pacific merchants of ancient trading routes and handicraftsmen.

Simultaneously, in emergent cities, science, philosophy, arts, and technologies started to arise. In urban environments, partially free from feudal and ecclesiastic control, and agrarian cycles, intellectuals recovered and developed classic knowledge, which was partially conserved by Arabs, then by Christian monks, and they enriched it with travel information. This activity emerged progressively from clandestinity, imposed by the Catholic Inquisition, mostly because the up-and-coming business and pre-industrial classes needed its scientific and technological results.

This intellectual drift[1] resulted in two central concepts - humanism and freedom. Over time, these have resulted in two more concepts, equality and "*progress*," which have led since the nineteenth century to "*economic growth*", "*development*", and "*egalitarianism*."

Expansion of trade, technology, manufacturing, and finance made possible a considerable improvement of material and welfare conditions, at least for the upper classes. After a primitive capital accumulation period came a full period of material growth. This was made possible by a massive military and colonial occupation of almost the entire world since the sixteenth century. European natural resources were eroded, but in the other continents, such oversized exploitation had never been done before. After genocidal and ethnocidal military conquest, European states transformed the colonial territories of Africa, Asia, America and Australia into extensive sources of food

1. We employ here the word *drift* in the same sense of French *dérive*, employed by Guy Debord and Situationism (Chollet, 2000) to conceptualise the method of getting and developing knowledge, and build up new situations, by existential, living, intellectual, artistic or travelling wandering. Concerning Renaissance period, Leonardo da Vinci life-story is paradigmatic of this practice.

and raw material, which was made possible by changes in local land and property use systems. Territories were considered the property of the colonial state, then distributed to European *colons* as private *latifundia*, or were directly plundered by the *colons* and crowds of European migrants.

In-kind or money taxes were imposed on smaller colonial or autochthonous farmers, grazers, and hunter-gatherers. Work was imposed on each individual and on entire nations in the forms of slavery, serfdom, and the starvation-wage proletariat, controlled by violence, manipulation, and cumulative debts with interest rates. Racist and civilizing ideologies gave moral support to this structure. Vast territories were deforested and converted into mono-agricultural or mono-forestry exploitation. Oversized mining, hunting, and fishing arose. This is the manner by which colonization destroyed most communitarian land use systems, as well as many production structures and knowledge that once allowed human societies to live in synergy with local ecosystems. Admittedly, this process also globalized many technologies, products, knowledge, and exchanges that improve human welfare (e.g., medicines, electricity, engines, science, and concepts like freedom and equality). But the subjacent sociopolitical structure, colonization, which carried the diffusion of these valuable improvements, had also disastrous ecological, social, and cultural consequences[1]

During this period, an idea took form gradually among Western philosophers, politicians and people. Apparently unlimited natural resources, increasing technology, and more efficient means of production made them conceive it would be possible to build an ever-growing universal and unlimited welfare by cumulative *material-economic growth*. This abstract path was called *progress*, or later on, *development*. And the way to build it was ever-increasing productivity to maximize the industrial production of objects. Despite Malthusian and other warning analyses, like the ones of the Rome Club, from the eighteenth century until the twentieth those concepts have become

1. This was not the colons' point of view. For instance, in 1756, in North-America, John Adams wrote: *"When colons arrived in America this continent was a continuous wild territory, home of wolves, bears and wild men. And now the forests are destroyed, land is covered by cultivated fields and by houses of civilized and educated people"* (Lopez, 1978).

a general representation (a faith) of the meaning of social activity, hence directed to the *future*. It is at this point that, among western or westernized people, time and life perceptions stopped being mainly cyclic and accessorily linear (elliptical), as with all living beings, to become chiefly linear, a race ahead to the *future*.[1]

However, independently of these industrialist ideological doctrines, growth is an intrinsic and structural need of new massive industrial-capitalist systems. Incessant global war among industrial-colonial states for territories, resources, workers, and markets requires an ever-growing military apparatus. Also, inside these societies, agricultural and industrial units fight for market control as a condition for survival. This competition is mainly determined by prices, an indicator of the supply and demand of merchandise, which determines the level of sales. This leads to an increasing productivity, obtained by more work, more automation, more consumption of natural resources, and violent or political control over markets and sources of raw materials. Among humans in these societies, the unlimited material richness of individuals or nations becomes a synonym for *success* of survival.

Within this sociocultural and production context, two superstructural questions had to be solved. Massive industrialization needed crowds of human workers, who would also be crowds of consumers, and it needed to feed them cheaply. This was solved by a simple strategy: a total deprivation of the rights of access and use of land and resources for most of the population, combined with an increase in food, raw materials and merchandise production.

I must mention that, in feudal societies, most of the population had the right to feed itself, even if landlords took a part - which varied from a tenth to one-third - of the production. In addition, large territories were commons, open to free use. Proteins were hoarded by the upper classes, who held monopolies on big game hunting and on weapons, but everyone could cultivate land, graze cattle, and gather food, water, firewood, and materials. This was seen as a natural right, restored by slavery's fall after the dissolution of the Roman Empire but it was also a duty imposed by the feudal rent systems.

---

1. The cultural nature of the concept of "*future*," in the sense described above, was put into relief in France in 2006 by several street political demonstrations demanding a "moratorium on the future" by putting an end to calendar accounting (Martí, 2007).

Those goals were reached by different policies, but they all followed the same underlying strategy. In England in the fourteenth century, landlords and monasteries gathered and *enclosed* peasant-rented lands, expulsed the tenants by violence, and replaced crop farming with sheep pastures to supply textile manufacturing. During the sixteenth century, the closing of monasteries resulted in land seizure by the rural bourgeoisie (*gentry*). At the same time, the profitability of wool induced the expansion of pasture enclosures. In the eighteenth century, by state policy, more than three thousand villages were enclosed and their lands gathered. Gentry and landlords rented out large plots to farmers; and their conjugated work built up intensive and new *high farming*. Throughout this long period, millions of people were expelled from their land; their villages were set on fire; and the former inhabitants were forced to migrate to industrial centers to work in factories and offices, in London, Liverpool and other growing cities. In the nineteenth century, national agriculture was no longer able to supply the growing urban demand, but protectionist *corn laws* sustained it, keeping prices high despite urban proletariat poverty. In 1849 corn laws were abolished by pressure from industrialists and land aristocracy. Agriculture was ruined, and the remaining farmers migrated to cities and colonies, but the industrial societal structure was achieved (Coulomb, 1994).

In France, such changes were made abruptly. During the 1789 French Revolution, peasants who rebelled *en masse* reclaimed the maintenance of communitarian land use systems, abolishment of feudal servitude, and reduced taxes. The 4th August 1789, the Constituent Assembly abolished feudalism. However, the overcoming industrial and business classes did not intend to distribute land and territory to the rural masses, not on an individual or on a collective basis. Ancient communitarian land use systems seemed backward to them.[1] They imposed the *private property* of land and resources, supported by ancient Roman law. This new legal feature was invented in the eighteenth century, and was defined by jurist Pothier in the triptych

1. Paradoxically, the peasant masses wished (e.g., in the *Carnets de Doléances* set everywhere in France by King Louis XVI during the first period of the French Revolution, so people could submit their complaints and demands) on one hand for the abolition of feudal servitude and a reduction in taxes and, on the other hand, for the conservation of "agrarian collective land uses of land, which have an essential role in their subsistence economy's precarious balance" (Coulomb, 1994).

"*Usus, Abusus, Fructus*." The goals of such policies are made explicit in debates from this period. For instance, in 1792 St. Just stated, "The cultivator…does not buy anything; his needs are not in trade." In 1793 Conventioneer Delacroix declared, "If we give the land to the people, we will not have a labour force" (for industry, agriculture and armies). During those years, new rulers violently repressed peasant movements for communitarian use of land. Gracchus Babeuf denounced "the false abolition of feudal regime."[1] He noticed the contradiction between the right to existence and this new property regime. His *Agrarian Programme* attempted to reclaim, among other things, "share of common lands not as property but by use," according to each region's communitarian traditions.[2] In 1797 Babeuf was condemned to death and executed, but the struggles of the French peasants remained throughout the nineteenth century. In 1804 the land private property rule was defined in Napoleon's Civil Code, which has been adopted and adapted by many States since the nineteenth century. By the new rule, a direct link between political power and property was avoided, eluding the contradiction between civil equality and property rights; all kinds of communitarian land use was forbidden, avoiding any return to a more "natural" state; land became a merchandise; farmers were forced to capitalize in order to get or to keep their livelihoods; intensive market-oriented production was increased; and most rural populations were deprived of land and resource use, becoming agricultural, industrial or soldier proletarians (Coulomb, 1994).

In all very industrialized countries, like in prior ones (e.g., England and France), the establishment of individual private land property preceded or coincided with the start of industrialization (Coulomb, 1994). The practice reached all Western countries, then other regions. For example, in 1874, forty-five percent of Portugal was still common land; presently, less than six percent remains common (Galhano Alves, 1994b; Rodrigues, 1987). In Leninist regimes, the same result was accomplished in a different way.

1. The private property of the territory was in contradiction with the Revolution axioms *Liberté, Égalité, Fraternité* (Freedom, Equality, Fraternity).
2. Consecutively, François-Noël ("Gracchus") Babeuf developed a collectivist totalitarian program and organized clandestine resistance in Paris, which had a strong influence on subsequent political movements (Buonarotti, 1828). His nickname may be related to the similarity between his own historical context and that of the Roman Graco's earlier democratic thinking (in the second century BC).

V

Dependence; Work; Money; Ever-Rising Growth

These processes caused a colossal migration on a scale never before seen in the History of humankind. Over the past few centuries, billions of people were deprived of their natural right to access and use land and vital natural resources. Hence, they became dependent on an exchange of merchandise to obtain food, energy, and welfare. As their only merchandise was themselves, they became a *proletarian*, dependent *workforce*. In such systems, the proletarians must *work* in industrial units (mostly in factories, offices and armies) in exchange for *money*, the universal abstract merchandise (Marx, 1883). They need to be *employed* by someone to do whatever, according to rigid timetables.

Hence, being *unemployed* means poverty, starvation, death, "survival incapacity," "social inadaptability"...It is at this point that *work*[1] becomes a social imposition, an abstract form of activity independent of a person's needs or will. As it is generalized and banal, atomized and militarized by its industrial chain social distribution, work destroys or subjugates all other kinds of social relationships.

1. Etymologically, in most European idioms, the concept of *work* expresses the activity of people without decision-making power (e.g., dependents, serfs, or slaves). Originally, the Germanic word *work* meant the forced activity of orphan children; Latin *laborare* meant the sufferings and humiliations of slaves; and Romanic *travail*, *trabajo*, and *trabalho* come from the Latin *tripalium*, a yoke employed to torture slaves and prisoners.

In hunting-gathering and agrarian societies, past and present, the labor force is used to accomplish concrete activities in time periods linked with natural cycles, individual or social needs, or impositions (Krisis, 1999).[1] Time used for production activities tends to be lower in communitarian societies[2] than in hierarchic slavery or feudal ones, which need large material accumulation. But in capitalist-industrial societies, work becomes an abstract, general activity, independent of its content or goal, culturally represented as morally valuable, and ultimately bound for endless accumulation of abstract capital (money)[3]. In this manner, dependence, work, money, and ever-rising growth have been interlinked into a unique social and cultural structure, shaping an anthropologic total social reality.

1. German philosophers from Krisis group state that "the history of the modern age is the history of the enforcement of labour [work], which brought devastation and horror to the Planet in its trail" (Krisis, 1999).
2. In India, Europe, and Africa, among people from semi-autarchic societies that maintain communitarian land use and family-based small farming, I noticed periods of more than eight hours a day of discontinuous production activity, but also others of two hours a day or less. Technically they don't have a work, but an activity.
3. This type of work may be called *wage slavery*.

VI

Leninism; Nazi Fascism; Democratic Socialism

Leninist *collectivist land property and use systems* resulted from several social and intellectual events. Karl Marx centered his economic growth theory on the fact that landowners' rent is made in detriment of farmers' profit, shortening investments for increasing productivity (Marx, 1883). In 1900, Kantsky, and later Lenin, thought that industrial and capital growth could happen only by ending land rent by elimination of private property. They deemed this meant nationalization and exploitation of the land by industrial farmers. Single-party dictatorship would nationalize territory easily, and so socialist state-capitalist systems would grow faster than the liberal-capitalist ones (Coulomb, 1994).[1] This policy was executed in the Soviet Union (USSR) after the October 1917 Russian Revolution, and in all Leninist countries - almost half the World in the second half of the twentieth century, in a high global historical speed of only 50 years. The Russian Revolution abolished slavery-like feudalism and nationalized land but, as in the former French Revolution, the new rulers did not give the land to the people. Since their beginnings, Leninist state land

1. These Leninist policies to implement massive industrial production were well depicted by Mao Tse-Tung in 1957, in his speech to the Chinese State Supreme Conference, in which he declared, "The achievement of agricultural cooperatives solved the big contradiction between socialist industrialization and individual agricultural economy…By the development of agriculture and cottage or basic industry, the heavy industry gets assured its markets and funds, and develops itself faster" (Tse-tung, 1969).

property systems evolved into collectivist industrial agricultural units, working as state enterprises or as collective cooperatives obeying to state planning (Lenin, 1923). Since the nineteenth century, in industrial countries, proletarian rebellions have strengthened, sustained by workers' "wage-slave" status. Lenin, based on Marxist analysis, envisaged state property and production planning as the "Proletarian Dictatorship," meant to direct to collective unlimited capital growth (*progress*) toward *total welfare* ("Communism"). To reach this abstract state in Leninist regimes, a totalitarian bureaucratic apparatus imposed planned, intensive industrialization, work and production, in industrial production centers, by means of ideological manipulation, violence, and compulsory population migrations. Throughout this period, from Siberia to Africa, many communitarian land use systems were destroyed. Since this over-tense structure collapsed in the 1980s and 1990s, the land is being privatized in Russia[1] and elsewhere by the State or by International Monetary Fund or World Bank impositions.[2]

In the twentieth century, in Europe (1922–1975)[3] and abroad, Nazi-Fascist totalitarian regimes set up *state corporatism*, an "alliance" among the state, large industrial groups, and agricultural *latifundia* landowners' groups, protecting each other's interests by patronage and violence. Dictatorship represses political or social opposition. Large private landowners keep territorial control on the rural workforce, with state support. Low wages and high rents result in high profits. Low prices of food and raw materials and low wages do support industrial and financial growth in favor of economic, political and military oligarchies (Coulomb, 1994). This selective social and militarized structure set the stage for capital growth, and when it was conjugated with nationalist racism, it resulted in slavery, plunder, expansionism, and genocide[4], all summarized in the Nazi axiom, "*Work liberates*" ("*Arbeit Match Frei*")[5]. In Europe and America, nazi-fascist regimes used all kinds of methods to destroy communitarian

1. Land privatization was legalized by the Russian parliament (*Duma*) the 26 June 2002, by a vote of 258 to 149.
2. More recently, in 2004, Robert Mugabe's totalitarian regime in Zimbabwe adopted a Leninist type of land property use by the state, nationalizing all the agricultural lands.
3. 1922 - Mussolini proclaims fascism in Rome. 1975 - Franco dies in Madrid.
4. Against Jews, Gypsies, communists, anarchists, socialists, homosexual, mental ill persons, etc.
5. The traditional speech, common to multiple peoples of the World, *"The one who doesn't work doesn't eat"* expresses a similar reading of the work.

territory use systems, for obvious reasons. For instance, Portuguese fascist dictatorship (1926 - 1974, the longest of the World) gave or sold common lands as private property; allowed the seizure of common land by local party bosses; and confiscated thousands of square kilometers of common land for timber industrial forestation (Galhano Alves, 1994b; Rodrigues, 1987).

In the early twentieth century Western Europe's democratic socialism theories, and later social-democracy systems, considered that "a peasant who labours his private land by his own work does not exploit anyone, being coherent with a Socialist society." This concept evolved into a Keynesian policy that favored *industrial family agriculture private land units*. State measures supported land ownership by farmers by minimizing rights and profits of renting through cost and price regulations, subventions, cooperative structures, and concentration of land property. Applied first in France and in the Benelux, this policy resulted in the present European Union agricultural system, which is intended to support delineated territorial, demographic, and industrial production structures. Since the 1960s, this policy has supported increased industrial agricultural productivity through mechanization and chemicals, resulting in high production, lower working costs, and lower prices for urban and international markets. Capital transferred to farmers by subventions keeps prices low and rural incomes high. Larger farmers get most of these subventions. The remaining small peasants are ruined and become proletarians (Coulomb, 1994). Industrial market-oriented agriculture ensures a permanent supply of low-cost food and raw materials for urban proletarian populations and for industry, thus avoiding an increase in wages and the subsequent decrease in capital growth. It also sustains an urban / rural demographic asymmetry, ensuring a workforce supply for industrial centers. Paradoxically, as agricultural over-intensification leads to overproduction of food and raw materials, causing the danger of falling prices and of ruining farmers, subventions are given to set aside a huge amount of farming land. Or subvention the destruction of a part of the crops. Besides that, subvention programs avoid territory over-depopulation. Presently, the "productivist" agricultural policies of other highly industrialized countries (e.g., the United States of America) are similar to those of European Union, even if other mechanisms are employed.

VII

Prohibitionist Societies; Homeostasis; Attachment Behavior; Ecological Unconscious

As we saw in the previous sections, throughout at least the last three millenniums, the abolition of communitarian territory use systems has been accomplished by different methods such as violent plunder, expropriation, or the subtle passage from a common status to a communal one, and then to a private one. This process, common to several civilizations, was particularly intensified in Europe, and then reached the entire World. Some present German philosophers call these two steps "internal colonization" followed by "overseas colonization" (Krisis, 1999). By those policies, the ancient oligarchic and the modern, highly industrialized capitalist societies, liberal or collectivist, deprived a majority of people from free access and use of territory and resources,[1] transforming them into a dependent labor force and consumers in order to survive. This permitted huge capital concentration and growth by intense exploitation of natural resources and work. Rising technologic development has also been used for this goal. But these three tools (e.g., territory and resource control, work, and technology) do not explain by themselves the formation of present massive consumption societies.

---

1. Therefore, all these societies should be called *prohibitionist societies* in terms of their superstructure, as they all are based on the interdiction for most individuals of the natural right to the autonomous use of territory and resources.

In fact, in such conditions it is technically possible to produce hundreds of millions of units of any sort of merchandise, such as little plastic zoomorphic objects. But this does not imply that people buy it. Therefore, a tendency toward unlimited consumption is an essential condition for the formation and existence of mass consumption societies, and it is linked with *attachment* behavior systems.

Human beings, like all animals, have three fundamentals homeostatic[1] behavior systems: the food and energy system, the attachment system, and the sexual system. Attachment behavior[2] generates and maintains the affective and linking proximity and communication among individuals of the same species. It is a fundamental behavior for the survival and evolution of many living species (Bowlby, 1973, Vols. I, III). But attachment also exists among individuals of different species (Galhano Alves, 1995, 2000, 2002, 2011, 2012). In all homeostatic behavior systems, the loss of goals generates stress and distress, activating incessant mechanisms to re-establish balance; these are primarily oriented to the access to food and energy, to the creation of intra-species[3] and inter-species[4] attachment relationships and links, and to sexual relationships and links (Bowlby, 1973, Vols. I, III).

Among human societies in close proximity to high or total biodiversity ecosystems, I have found a strong attachment toward the biologic, natural, environment, as is shown in several cases. Among the people of the Sariska Tiger Reserve region, in India, eighty-eight percent of their free drawings represent wild or domestic animals and plants, and only twelve percent represent humans or artificial objects. Wildlife is also omnipresent in their dreams, daily aesthetical contemplation of nature, daily behavior, speech, and religious, cultural and cognitive representations. In the magico-religious sphere, they

1. *Homeostasis* is a property of either an open system or a closed system, especially a living organism that regulates its internal environment in order to maintain a stable, constant condition. Multiple dynamic equilibrium adjustments and regulation mechanisms (control systems) make homeostasis possible. The concept was created by French Doctor Claude Bernard (1865). He also stated that "constancy of the internal environment is the condition for a free and independent life."
2. Attachment behavior systems have been described and studied by the British psychoanalyst and ethologist John Bowlby since 1948.
3. Among members of the same species.
4. Among members of different species.

use to draw animals, like tigers, panthers or birds in the walls of the ancient Hindu temples in the jungle. They say they do this “because animals have many beauty”, and to “protect the cattle”.

“Tiger” – Free drawing of a herder of Gurjar tribe, Mr. Um Rao Gurjar, in Haripura village, in the Sariska Tiger Reserve (Rajasthan, India), 1994. The inhabitants represent mostly aspects of Nature in their free drawings, and Nature is also very present in their night dreams and other aspects of their inner life. What indicates a well-developed ecological unconscious, in an ecosystem in the state of total biodiversity, including tigers - Collection: Museu de História Natural e da Ciência da Universidade do Porto (Portugal). Given by J.P. Galhano Alves.

The same happens in W National Park region, in Niger, among human societies within the lions’ savannah.

This strong inter-species attachment to each particular living being and feature, to the whole biologic universe, to the whole environment and landscape, configures what I call the *ecological unconscious*. The ecological unconscious is a part of the psyche, different from the personal unconscious and from the collective one; but the three are structurally interdependent. It is aimed at and results

"Elefant, bird heron, palm tree and the empty space, by night" – Free drawing by a 44 years old man of the Moli Haoussa(-Gourma) village, in the region of W National Park (Niger), 2002. The elements of Nature are dominant in the free drawings of the region' inhabitants. What indicates a well-developed ecological unconscious, in an ecosystem in state of total biodiversity, including lions - Collection: Museu de História Natural e da Ciência da Universidade do Porto (Portugal). Given by J.P. Galhano Alves.

in the creation of links among each individual and the other living beings. These links create an unconscious knowledge of the living that successively shapes behavior as well as symbolic, cognitive, and complex forms. Ecological unconscious attachment behavior systems exist in all living beings, but its normal development needs proper environmental and sociocultural conditions. Its universal existence in the human species is affirmed by common attachments to animals and plants, natural features, natural processes, and landscapes (also called "biophilia"). More evidence of the ecological unconscious attachment behavior system is demonstrated by the universal presence of those natural elements, since Paleolithic times, in cultural, religious, and aesthetic representations - literature and art.[1] Accomplishment of inter-

1. Presently, millions of persons, from urban minimal biodiversity regions, travel each year to high biodiversity regions in order to *"contact with Nature"*. Tourists who travel thousands of kilometres to spend some days at Sariska Tiger Reserve, in India,

species attachment is an intrinsic and fundamental factor for individual and collective homeostasis and welfare. Obviously, inter-species attachment is totally possible in total or high biodiversity humanized ecosystems, as it is shown in the examples above (Galhano Alves, 1995, 2000, 2002, 2011, 2012).

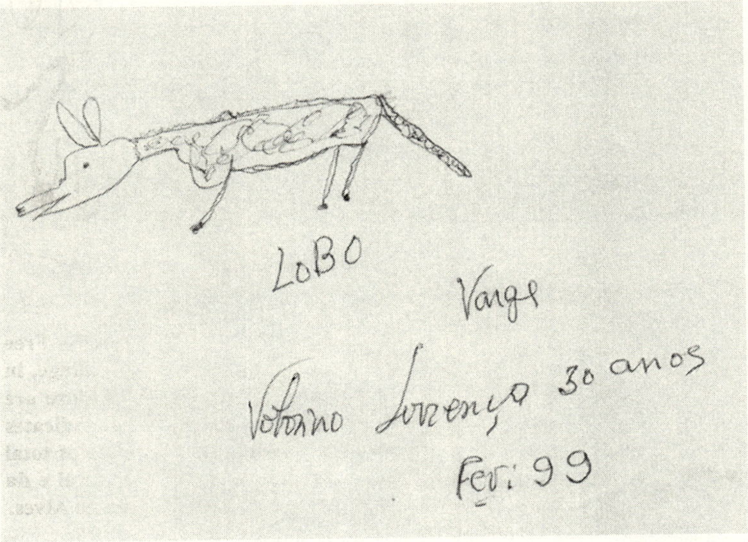

"Wolf" - Free drawing of Mr. Vitorino Lourenço, 30 years old, inhabitant of the Varge village, in Montesinho Natural Park (North-East of Portugal), February 1999. A representation coming from the ecological unconscious, in this ecosystem in state of high biodiversity, including wolves - Collection: Museu de História Natural e da Ciência da Universidade do Porto (Portugal). Given by J.P. Galhano Alves.

But in such environments, cultural factors may also inhibit inter-species attachment or alter it selectively. For instance, I noticed that among people from the North-East of Portugal, free drawings represent mostly village scenes, houses and people, despite their close coexistence with a rich wildlife. Negative cultural representations of nonhuman life resulted in a partial repression and inhibition of

use to say they did it just to *"see animals"*. This is also evidence of the existence of the inter-specific attachment behaviour and the ecological unconscious (Galhano Alves, 1995, 2000, 2002).

inter-species attachment, and in an absorption of the peasant universe into itself. This has negative repercussions on local cognitive representations of nature, on people's relationships with several species, and on the relationship with their ecosystem.[1] Yet, as a whole, they maintain the attachment to their natural landscape (Galhano Alves, 1995, 2002, 2003, 2012).

Thus, in total or high biodiversity humanized ecosystems, where close, multiple, and daily interaction with wildlife takes place, inter-species attachment behavior may achieve satisfactory homeostatic levels. At the same time, in this type of rural human community, family and solidarity interactions tend to be predominant, improving possibilities for intra-species attachment behavior homeostasis. They are societies in which loneliness does not exist.

When communitarian territory use and family land use systems are predominant, as they are in these societies, the free access to vital resources is ensured to each individual. This freedom supports homeostasis of the food and energy behavior system, which just has to activate the necessary processes and actions in space and time to acquire and keep food, water, combustible materials, and row materials to make houses or tools, that are accessible in nearby areas. Gifts and trade may provide exchanges of supplemental vital or luxurious things.

For these reasons, in communitarian land use societies within total or high biodiversity ecosystems, both food and energy, and attachment behavior systems lend a normal and favorable support to homeostasis. In fact, among these societies, distress or conflict is mostly caused by the sexual behavior system, caused from processes such as falling in love, marriage, or sociocultural repressive gender discrimination structures, and also by attachment loss caused by death (mourning). Therefore, stress stays at a low, periodical, and natural level. This is well expressed by a young Gurjar tribal man from the Sariska Tiger Reserve region (Rajasthan, India) who says, "I love Gurjar life. Because I have food, I have milk, I live in the jungle and I do not have too much work."

---

1. An extreme case of selective inter-species attachment occurs in Castilla (Spain). For some obscure reason, local populations wiped out all trees except those of a single species, *Quercus ilex* (Holm oak) (Galhano Alves, 2000, 2002).

VIII

Stress; Distress; Employment; Unemployment; Hierarchy; Competition

"(I Can't Get No) Satisfaction." - Mick Jagger and Keith Richards, The Rolling Stones - Hollywood, California, USA, 1965

These balances cannot happen, or may happen only with difficulty, in urban or agrarian low or minimal biodiversity ecosystems and in prohibitionist land use systems, such as the ancient oligarchic or the present capitalist (liberal or collectivist) societies. In fact, in very urbanized or very eroded agrarian environments, huge masses of people have been disconnected from Nature and biodiversity. The massive migration of the last centuries, caused by the political processes described above, resulted in concentrationist urbanism and the present territorial demographic imbalance. Now in highly industrialized countries, about eighty percent of people inhabit in urban areas. The global urban population comprises more than fifty percent of humanity.[1] Most people live in a megalopolis of some sort. In such minimal biodiversity and abiotic environments, those populations have very low, poor chances to direct their inter-species attachment toward biological organisms, vegetation and fauna, or to natural features. Therefore, inter-species attachment is in permanent *stress*. Mechanisms to re-establish homeostasis are permanently activated,

1. Data extrapolated from 1995 World Bank demographic statistics.

but they can never reach their goal as it does not exist in such artificial environments. Consequently, transference mechanisms of defense are overactivated, leading to ever-growing attachment behavior toward the things that exist in such environments (i.e. toward their elements). These are mostly objects, images, and abstract features, which cannot bring real homeostasis to the attachment system. Massive inter-species attachment to pets, two-dimensional audiovisual documentaries on Nature, or vacation travel to natural regions may reduce such distress, but cannot end it in the daily existence of most people, primarily at the unconscious level. The same is true concerning the existence of a few urban public gardens.

An agrarian industrial minimal biodiversity ecosystem. In this case, the level of biodiversity is only of one species (Olive tree – Olea *europaea*) in an area of hundreds of square Km. Great amounts of work, energy and chemical products are needed to keep it. Its productivity is only apparent and no sustainable, and it is much lower than the one of total or high biodiversity humanized ecosystems. Andalucia, Spain, Iberia, European Union, years 1990. Photo © J.P. Galhano Alves.

In these societies the free access to vital and natural resources does not exist for most people, because of land property regimes, plus physical distance. The survival of the inhabitants of these societies depends on obtaining abstract exchange merchandise (*money*) to buy food and energy, things and habitats. The lack of direct contact or free access to vital resources, as well as the uncertainty and randomness of obtaining money, produce permanent *stress* and *distress* of the food and energy behavior system. Paradoxically, to obtain money and vital items, people must submit their time and labor by being *employed.* This naturally increases their stress or, inversely, makes them feel proud of being employed by ideological manipulation and self-suggestion. Alternatively, they must steal those vital items, which is also a stressing situation. In such circumstances, individuals logically link *unemployment* or *bankrupt* with poverty, misery, and sociocultural inferiority. At an unconscious level those concepts represent *death*, leading to extreme distress. For these reasons, mechanisms of defense are permanently overactivated for the exponential accumulation of money and merchandisable objects, which may procure present and future "security" and social status.

Finally, in such societies the absolute dependency of the individual on indirect, uncertain, and random ways to obtain resources varies as a function of each person's rank in social *hierarchy* (e.g., peasant, vagrant, not-proletarian, proletarian, unemployed, employed, low waged, upper waged, subordinated, superior, boss, capitalist, citizen, ruling-party member, military, or ruler). For this reason, *competition* becomes the center of social activity; competition for resources, work, and money. Thus, in prohibitionist, oligarchic, or capitalist (liberal or collectivist) societies, competition among individuals, production units, and social groups invades all spheres of individual and social behavior, handicapping intra-species attachment. This configures an implosive social structure. Competition prevails upon synergy, association, attachment, and alliance relationships, contrary to what is normal in all other animal, primate, hominid, and human societies. The intra-species attachment system becomes overstressed, and mechanisms of defense are permanently overactivated, making transferences by increasing competition; attachment to objects, images, or abstract features; or by turning aggressiveness into oneself. Competition for work, money, productivity, consumption, and social rank overcomes honesty, sincerity, solidarity, and intra-species attachment. Aggressiveness, violence, loneliness, stress, and distress become general, resulting in a collective agitation state. Overactivity and depression become pandemic. Suicide also becomes usual.

Humans and other primates have always used psychotropic drugs for spiritual, intellectual, therapeutic, or ludic purposes; but in such competitive sociopsychological structures, pandemic psychotropic drugs overconsumption, legal or illegal, becomes crucial for the artificial increase or decrease of dopamine, adrenaline and endomorphine hormones levels.

The cult of competition becomes massive in many forms, including mass sporting matches. Attachment frustration results in transference by oral, sexual, or aggressiveness malfunctions. Social or arbitrary violence and corruption becomes common.

In such conditions, a huge and expensive armed police and prison apparatus appears as a violent system of control to avoid total social implosion of these anonymous mass societies.[1] Furthermore, violent competition among states, industry, finance, and political groups results in a continuous state of nomadic global war for control of resources, people, and markets, requiring an ever-growing huge military apparatus, which may lead to global implosion.

1. Concerning this aspect, Herbert Marcuse pointed out their condition of "societies under control" (Marcuse, 1976).

IX

Objects, Images, and Abstract Features; Boredom; Simulacrum of Activity; Simulacrum of Life; Simulacrum World; Massive Production and Consumption Societies; Societies of Objects

Fundamentally, in such social structures and in minimal or low biodiversity environments, inter-species and intra-species natural attachment behavior is not able to accomplish homeostasis, or has many difficulties in doing so. This results in incessant overactivation of mechanisms of defense to re-establish balance, which leads, in such conditions, to attachment transference mainly toward *objects*, *images*, and *abstract features*, which are the more easily accessible things in such environments. This results in exponential consumption of those items. In those societies such items are produced as merchandises, which supports intrinsic, ever-growing industrial production and capital growth. But such items by themselves are not able to satisfy the natural human attachment and existential behavior needs, which evolved through time in very different natural and social environments (Galhano Alves, 1995, 2002, 2009a, 2012, 2021, 2023). Thus, massive *boredom* becomes chronic, increasing mass consumption, agitation, violence, and depression (Vaneigem, 1999).

A minimal biodiversity tecno-industrial abiotic urban ecosystem. In a permanent Brownian activity to reproduce and increase abstract capital money. Europe, 2021. Photo © J.P. Galhano Alves.

Therefore, attachment frustration is a structural and dynamic support of massive production and consumption societies, along with territory control and intensive exploitation of natural resources, work, and technology (Galhano Alves, 1995, 2002, 2009a, 2021, 2023). The first condition for the existence of such societies is the destruction of all links between man and Nature (Debord, 1967).

Moreover, boredom is also linked with the conditions in which human production activity has been transformed into an impersonal and repetitive behavior by productivist work chain distribution[1] in factories, offices, and industrial farms. Sigmund Freud pointed out the virtues of work (i.e., human productive activity directed toward a goal) and its importance for psycho-physiological balance when it is freely chosen, and hence engages one's personality. But in such production systems the work is not freely chosen for most people (Friedman, 1963; Marx, 1872 - 1875, in Marglin et al., 1974). Leroi-Gourhan (1965) also noticed the inadaptability of human psycho-physiology to such techno-industrial production systems. Distress becomes intrinsically linked to what should be a vital and creative, individual and social, productive activity. For most people, work has become an activity separated from their wills, needs or talents, a compulsory way to obtain a wage in money.[2] Their lives are outside work, during "free time." Production units must use all kinds of control, manipulation, and recompensing methods to keep up productivity,[3] and competition plays also its role (Friedman, 1963). Therefore, from an existential point of view, for most people work and production activities become what I call a *simulacrum of activity*.

And, also, because most attachment and consumption behaviors are directed by transference mechanisms toward artificial objects, images, and abstract features made to balance boredom, and this occurs inside highly artificial environments, the existence of most people has become what I call a *simulacrum of life*, in a *simulacrum world*.

In such social and psychological environments, it is not surprising that many economists postulate that "human needs are unlimited." This is one of the abstract but fundamental premises of economy studies.

It is also in such environments that, since the twentieth century, modern nonfigurative abstract art developed as a common manifestation of human absorption into its own artificial, abstraction-

1. In the USA, in XXth century, Frederick W. Taylor's methods of work management in chain increased these alien, monotonous, military features.
2. Karl Marx noticed that the forced worker "feels like being at home outside the work, and outside himself in the work…hence work is not the fulfillment of a need, but only a means to fulfill needs outside of it. One proof of its alien character towards the worker is the fact that since the moment physical or another kind of coercion cease to exist, one runs away from work as from pest" (quoted in Krisis, 1999).
3. This is particularly visible in Leninist systems, in which compulsory work is rewarded with "productivity recompenses" and "work hero awards." In "liberal" capitalist enterprises, similar methods are employed.

born world, while surrealism used figurative art to picture the human existential and inner world remaining under *unbiotical* urban structures. Subsequently, pop art depicted itself as merchandise.

Herbert Marcuse classified these societies as *mass consumption* ones, during a stage when massive production and consumption were mostly oriented toward objects and tools. But growth in consumption is not only quantitative, but also qualitative. In its first nineteenth and twentieth centuries phases, massive industrial production did generalize many useful objects, products, and tools. Industrial production at that point was still oriented toward useful needs that improved welfare. It inherited and reproduced the handicraft and manufacturing traditions, making durable, functional, or sophisticated products. It is true that the way in which production rates, transport, and energy and resource consumption were organized was already ecologically unsustainable. But its outcomes have been, and still are, a crucial factor in the welfare of the human species. This is obvious for all people and civilizations, even in the remotest villages, which may now use bicycles, motor vehicles, water pumps, biochemical medicines, sewing machines, and many other items[1].

Presently, different phases of consumption behavior are co-mingled around the globe. During the twentieth century, radio and cinema reached almost all the World. Since the 1960s daily mass consumption of images and sounds has become a reality, with television spreading in both highly industrialized and not-industrialized countries. Also, during the nineteenth and twentieth centuries, mass consumption of all kinds of items raised. Beyond a certain level, it does not matter anymore what is produced and consumed, or how it is produced, or for what purpose. Enterprises and entire nations need to endlessly produce more merchandise and sell it faster to maintain markets, work, and capital growth. Dependent masses are susceptible to all kinds of manipulating propaganda, called "marketing," and intrinsically always need more consumption. In this running-ahead process, any unit of merchandise is a "good, as economists say."[2] All quality, durability

1. The Mahatma ("Big-Soul") Gandhi said that the best heritages of India from the British Empire were the railway and the sewing machines.
2. According to economic theories, everything that may be merchandised, except work, is a "good." Land, water, living beings, manufactured and industrial objects, and even grenades and bombs, are "goods."

and usefulness decrease. This erosion affects all sectors of the society, including intellectual, cultural, teaching, and research activities, which by mimicry submit to the crowd's competitive productivity rate. As well, high quality, natural food and merchandise become rare and expensive, generating a growing but restricted market.

And, mostly, audiovisual merchandise rises. These products are the ones that fill up the two principal human senses, vision and audition, creating an almost total simulation of in-motion reality and a hypnotic-like effect. Hence, audiovisual merchandise is very apt to diminish boredom and to support behavior transference mechanisms. The relative production cost is cheap, as each product reaches millions of people; the consumption cost of audiovisual merchandise is also very cheap. Endless production and consumption of television and other audiovisual merchandise results in an ever-renewed variety of simulated and media-driven virtual reality, which configures an alien but present world. This one tends to be "perfect," as it is always readapted to the spectators' wishes in order to be sold. Huge audiences live part of their daily lives absorbed in this audiovisual world. Therefore, television never stops.

Simulation needs to permanently increase in intensity to be effective and stimulating, reaching spectacular levels. This context of widespread simulation of activity, life, and reality itself among mass consumption societies has led Guy Debord (1967, 1988) to classify them as *societies of the spectacle*. But basically, they remain *prohibitionist-based societies of mass production and consumption of objects, images, and abstract features*, which I call, more simply, *societies of objects* (Galhano Alves, 1995, 2002, 2009, 2021, 2023).

X

Dependency Status; Conditioning

By now we have seen how most people in societies of mass production and consumption (societies of objects) became almost totally dependent on work, money and consumption in order to fulfill their food, energy and attachment needs. Or, in other words, how most territory and lands, natural resources, food, raw materials, people, and things have become merchandise and tools for the growth of production and capital. This *dependency status* is not only the condition of proletarians; it is the main condition of the whole social superstructure, which concerns all individuals. All are interdependent, including market-oriented landowner' farmers, industry owners, and businessmen. Marxist and Leninist "class struggle" analysis did not take in account such structural interdependency, resulting in a simple change of the oligarchy that controls resources and work, maintaining mass dependence for capital growth. It even increases mass dependency and submission through "Proletariat Party Dictatorship," which means the abolition of democratic civil rights and individual freedoms.

After several generations of urban life in abiotic environments, most humans do not know anymore how to survive by themselves. They do not know how to cultivate land, grow crops, make and use tools, raise cattle, gather, fish, hunt, or build houses or other vital structures. Neither do they know how to manage and use natural resources to provide vital and superfluous needs, nor how to live within natural environments. Living in total or high biodiversity requires large amounts of technique and knowledge that was developed over the course of millenniums. Human inhabitants of biodiverse ecosystems even know how to react safely when one encounters a tiger, a lion, or a grizzly bear (Galhano Alves, 1995, 1999, 2002, 2007a, 2007b, 2012; Galhano Alves & Garcia-Perea, 1998).

Chain atomization of productive activity has led to individual loss of knowledge and skills. Most people in societies of objects are unable to perform all the steps needed to manufacture handicrafts (e.g., carpentry, masonry, pottery, metallurgy, textile manufacturing, or other handicraft technology). This loss of knowledge and skill includes techniques that were once common to all humans, distinctive skills of the species; for instance, very few modern humans or human groups know how to produce fire by themselves.[1]

Therefore, a massive and historically very quick loss of knowledge has taken place. In direct contrast with what was the norm through all epochs and civilizations, presently the basic and detailed information, techniques, and systems that were developed by mankind to survive and to adapt to natural landscapes, to use and manage resources, to improve living conditions, has become unknown or unusual for most people. More and more of these skills are disappearing forever, as the remaining people or human groups who still know them are absorbed by industrial structures, undergo environmental change, are destroyed by *wilderness policies* in protected territories, or just vanish.

Paradoxically, within the simulacrum world, on one hand scientific data and knowledge increases; industrial technology rises; and an ever-growing amount of information, data, and news on all topics and matters is permanently propagated by media, education, and informatics channels, reaching almost everywhere. But on the other hand, the range of techniques, skills, and knowledge effectively known by individuals decreases, reaching a bottom level in which inhabitants, engaged in a simulacrum of life, are unable to ensure either their own existence or that of their nearby group.

1. Presently, the villagers from W National Park region (Niger) are among of the rare examples of people still able to produce fire by themselves. They light it by striking sparks from a jasper hard-stone using a tempered iron handle, which lights a bit of wild vegetable wool, then dried brushwood. But they do not light it by knocking two stones together. They may also produce fire by friction between two wooden sticks (Galhano Alves, 2012).

In societies of objects, the *dependent status* of most people results from deprivation from free access to vital and natural resources, owing to the barriers of land property regimes as well as a significant physical distance from the resources. But the dependence of these people is also linked with the fact that they do not know how to exist outside the economic and environmental structures of the simulacrum world.

Having been formed throughout their lifetimes and over the course of several generations inside the simulacrum world, the behavior systems of the human inhabitants are configured to adapt to it. Individual skills are formed to survive there, to be able to do a specific range of actions and tasks that fit into artificial, urbanized environments and into a mass chain production network, which requires always more specialized capability. In addition, attachment behavior becomes dependent on permanent and varying consumption. Values and cultural representations become mimicry of this human-made, abiotic, competitive, material, and abstract background. Most of these skills, behaviors and values are useful or make sense only as they fit into the background of the simulacrum world. But as these influences shape and fulfill essential parts of each individual's existence, they tie people to the whole mass production and consumption structure by an intrinsic dependency on it. Hence, most people become intrinsically dependent on urbanized and abiotic environments, and on the triptych of work, money, and consumption.

The fact that each individual and his nearby group have become unable to survive by themselves implies a deep intrinsic dependency status. I must say that, as John Bowlby pointed out, "dependency" indicates the degree to which an individual is subordinated to another one in order to secure his survival. Dependency is absolute at the moment of birth and decreases more or less gradually until maturity (Bowlby, 1973, Vol. I). In fact, in humans, as with all primates, mammals, and other classes and species, dependency is mostly the status of young, immature, individuals who are unable to ensure their survival and autonomous life.[1] The ones who are dependent are the children.

1. Childhood and puberty are the most dependent phases of life. Normally, human puberty ends between the ages of 13 and 15 (Bühler, 1962).

Thus, in the simulacrum world, each individual's condition of practically total dependency corresponds to a growing phenomenon of mass infantilism.

This dependence leads to a high collective susceptibility to behavior conditioning, manipulation, and control. As most people became individually and structurally dependent, on the industrial simulacrum world, their vital and attachment needs can't be satisfied except by indirect ways entailing work, money, and consumption, by which they can get merchandise to survive and balance boredom. Moreover, as a simulacrum of life is commonly imbibed through simulated and virtual activities and realities, these products must be endlessly refined, and their spectacular effects endlessly improved, in order to be effective. Single changes in the content and parameters of such realities may act as a metamorphosis of the whole reality. In such contexts, all kinds of *conditioning* techniques become effective for huge masses of people.

It is known that, among humans as in other animal species, conditioning may be done by imprinting and by reaction to negative or positive conditioning stimuli, natural or formed, which reinforces a particular reactive or operative behavior. Such modifications in the behavior tendencies of individuals may be formed by repetition of the conditioning stimulus until the intended behavior is learned and executed in a particular situation. A conditioned behavior may also be erased by stopping the repetition of its conditioning stimulus. The effectiveness of conditioning depends mostly on motivation and on stimulation frequency. Motivation is higher when a positive conditioning stimulus satisfies a need, balancing a deprivation state. These processes may also be used in complex sequences, conditioning several and successive reactions or operations over time, molding behavior toward a specific goal. In addition, negative stimuli, which produce escaping and avoidance conditioned reactions, may be used as punishment to decrease or stop unwanted behaviors. Obviously, conditioned behavior is incorporated and accepted by individuals better when molding, rather than aversive, techniques are used (Landauer, 1972).

Thus, we may see how susceptible human beings can be to conditioning by these, or other more sophisticated methods, in the above-described economic and artificial structures of the simulacrum world. Conditioning is a basic mechanism for learning among children and mature individuals alike. Normally it is more effective on children, as they are in a learning and dependent, developing, phase, lacking a wide range of references. Nevertheless, within those societies the ever latent and real possibility of deprivation of vital or superfluous needs produces dependency, stress, and distress, facilitating the use of positive or negative stimuli in order to control the behavior of the whole society. Moreover, the collective permanent need to consume objects and an ever-renewed variety of simulated or media-driven virtual reality, which may diminish boredom and support attachment behavior transference mechanisms, submerges individuals in a false reality. This false reality is in permanent metamorphosis, because to be effective it must be in constant motion[1] and even more spectacular than the real living world itself - even if its movement and spectacular effects are a simulation, happening in an unchanging and monotonous substrate of inert artificial structures, objects, images, and sounds.

For these reasons, in the societies of objects, the collective dependency status and the immersion in a human-made, unnatural, and simulated reality facilitate mass manipulation and control. In fact, mass manipulation and control might be an intrinsic requirement of such social structures. Work and competition are at the core of social activity, subjugating all other kinds of social relationships. Thus, social cohesion and direction cannot be achieved without methods of mass control and simulated goals, which must be spectacular enough to pull together huge crowds of people. Without some kind of social cohesion and direction, the risk of social implosion or untidy drift becomes greater.

This manipulated and, to a large degree, simulated dynamic is reflected both in everyday life and in mass social events. Conditioning molding methods may be used by ruling groups in sophisticated ways. During the European Middle Ages, the powers and the Catholic Church disseminated terror sentencing to dead hundreds of thousands of "witches" and wolf-man". During the 1930's and till 1945, German and Austrian Nazism used Jews as targets of the collective violence.

1. As Landauer (1972) pointed out, "apparently animals and humans prefer a world where little changes that do not scare anybody take place and not a world where everything is always constant."

Also, during the twentieth century, Leninist regimes often employed molding methods to manipulate collective aggressiveness toward an intended target. For instance, in 1968, the democratization process in Czechoslovakia, the so-called Prague Spring, was suppressed by Soviet Union (USSR) and Warsaw Pact armies on the night of 20th to 21st August, putting an end to Alexander Dubcek's leadership. New rulers, headed by Gustav Husák, achieved military control of the country, but it was difficult to gain total social control, as the whole nation was against the occupation regime and had lost faith in communism. To purge opposing individuals and groups, the ruling party needed loyal people who could relay power, aggressiveness, and terror among the population. Such conditioned aggressive and persecution behaviors were formed by a complex two-step method. As Kundera (1983) points out, first the ruling party organized a media campaign against (provisional) nonhuman living targets to which people normally have strong attachment links: animals and pets. Newspapers published countless articles and letters demanding the extermination of doves in the towns, and doves really were exterminated. But the main targets of the campaign were the dogs. Despite the military occupation, newspapers, radio, and television promoted the idea that dogs were unhygienic for streets and public gardens, dangerous for public health, useless and, moreover, must be fed. People began persecuting dogs. One year later, when collective aggressiveness was entrenched and reached psychotic levels, "It was pointed at its real target: men. Dismissals, arrests and trials began" (Kundera, 1983).

Identical methods have been employed in Soviet Union (USSR) (with dogs). In China, during the Maoist "cultural revolution" (1966–1976), fear of microbes was disseminated, stimulating suspicion and persecution behavior. During this period, Beijing students put on medical masks before dancing together at parties, to avoid the danger of invisible microbes, while, as "red guards," they searched, denounced, killed, or led to suicide the "hidden revolution enemies", their "old habits" and "the traditions"[1].

Endless examples of this kind of social conditioning can be found in contemporary mass societies, whether they are collectivist or liberal,

1. Mao Tse-Tung, in the beginning of the Cultural Revolution, gave the order to the young people to "destroy the traditions".

totalitarian or pluralist. During the Cold War period, the state of fear and alert among the population of the United States of America was heightened by a media campaign warning of a spurious "imminent killer-bees deadly invasion." At the same time, Albania's Tirana radio broadcast weekly false reports on armed invasion attempts against the country. More recently, between 2001 and 2005, global broadcasting led almost all humans, at least during several months, to believe that "massive destruction weapons" were ready to be used from the Middle East against the rest of the World. Similarly, the global alert on avian flu, made first by the U.S.A. government and a few biomedical researchers and fuelled by the media, led to a global mass elimination of chicken and birds - just before the massive bombing of Lebanon in 2006. Maybe these two last examples have no rapport with the former ones, but in a simulacrum world, truth and lies no longer have a borderline.

In such contexts, it is possible to maintain global masses of people in a never-ending simulacrum of reality, as reality itself becomes purely abstract, in a world that is perceived in virtual and deliberately manipulated ways. Such a succession of spectacular simulacrums takes possession of all dimensions of individual and collective lives, shaping a drift toward a break between human dynamics and the real world. The break is shared by leading classes and political powers.

XI

"No future." - Simon John Ritchie ("Sid Vicious") and The Sex Pistols (England, twentieth century)

Since computer language became dominant in the last quarter of the twentieth century, a very important part of the interactions among humans have been reduced to combinations of the numbers 0 (zero) and 1 (one), which form the basis of the language of informatics. This is not surprising, because as interactions increase, language must become more basic and also more abstract, taking into account that the zero and the one numbers are probably the primary abstract concepts ever conceived by the human species.

Trade exchanges are also mostly processed in such basic language. This can be seen particularly in stock exchange markets, where a never-ending drift of numeric combinations substitute real merchandise production and exchange. It is very doubtful that the huge number of numeric combinations made in such markets, and in the other spheres of human life, still fit with social and natural realities. In fact, it is more probable that such successions of abstract realities no longer have any meaning, being based, more than on reality, on an abstract world build up by itself. In this point, we may consider that economic abstractions are self-made, without having correspondence to real natural resources, productive activities, or real human needs. In abstract trade, where abstract numbers multiply themselves in a succession of abstract and random ever-growing combinations, *money* becomes an entity that increases or decreases in trade value according, exclusively, to the random succession of virtual informatics operations that are made at almost light speed, using electromagnetic waves. Presently, in a single instant, an incalculable number of operations are made in such a way, without any logical pattern. If such numeric combinations stop, all virtual "economic reality" will fall off, and the whole social and productive structure, as we know it presently, would collapse.

As we saw before, never-ending capital growth is an intrinsic requirement of such social and productive systems. If in its beginnings such growth was based almost exclusively on exploitation of natural resources, work, and consumption, in its present virtual status it has become almost purely abstract, distancing itself from the real status of resources, work, or consumption. In other words, money no longer has a parallel with merchandise production or exchanges; it started simply reproducing itself, obeying the structural intrinsic need of capital growth.

Does this socioeconomic dynamic have a limit? Such limits cannot come from within the dynamic, as it fuels itself on a virtual basis. External factors may put an end to it; reality is far removed from the virtual world and from its spectacular effects, even if they almost substitute reality among most modern populations. In fact, abstract capital growth cannot surpass a certain border, the one on which it reveals its purely abstract and false reality. Exploitation of resources, work, and merchandise production, even if it is purely virtual, needs to keep rising, if only for the sake of being a pale evidence of money's value and growth.

Even supposing that work and abstract exchanges can last forever, this is not the case with natural resources, which are reaching an end. Living species, agricultural soils, drinking and irrigation water, rough materials, and energy are reaching their limits of possible exploitation;[1]

1. Living species are vanishing at an average rate of one species every eight minutes. About twenty-five percent (25%) of the species that existed in the 1970s are already extinct (but many other species vanished before, since the eighteenth century), and about twenty-five percent (25%) of the remaining species are expected to become extinct in the next few decades. This means that about one half of the World's living species have already disappeared or will vanish within a very short period of about 250 years.

nature cannot support the growing human superstructure. Pollution grows along with exploitation, production, and consumption, causing

---

A Big Extinction, like the one that ended with the Secondary Period, with dinosaurs very fast vanishment, and the passage to the Third Period of life on Earth, with the domination by mammal's species. And, more than fifty millions of years ago, the passage to the Fourth Period, with the expansion and multiplication of human populations, making the World' ecosystems becoming almost all humanized ecosystems. These were originally in a total biodiversity state. But today, with the vanishment or regression of about one half of the living species, the regression of human cultures that live in balance with Nature, and the expansion of tecno-industrial exploitation of Nature, total biodiversity humanized ecosystems are few and isolated in the World.

The growing destruction of biodiversity, biotopes and entire global ecosystems, started mostly in the beginning of Industrial Era, since late XVIIIth century.

The rate of this new Big Extinction, caused by human structures and activities linked with dominant societies, is so high that I think that we are in a fast passage to a new *Fifth Period*, where ecosystems will be poor, and humanity too. Maybe we are already in this new *Fifth Paleontological Period*. And all the remaining living species, including humans, must adapt to this new situation in order to survive. As the North American Native Sioux nation great Chief, Mr. Sitting Bull, stated in the XIXth century, "life ends and survival begins".

Moreover, more than sixty percent (60%) of the world's forests have been already destroyed. Arable soils are regressing by erosion; twenty percent (20%) of the arable soil that existed in 1990 were gone in 2010.

Water consumption is increasing, even if humanity already consumes more than thirty percent (30%) of the exploitable resources in inhabited zones.

The seas are becoming saltwater deserts; over the past few decades, one third (1/3) of the natural fish production has been consumed every year.

The planet's atmosphere is heavily polluted: In addition to other toxic gases, CO_2 levels have already increased more than thirty percent (30%) since 1860, causing an increase of more than 1°C on global atmospheric temperature since 1880. This leads also to a growing succession of climate disasters, like floods, cyclones, dryness, etc. This leads also to an expected increase of about 1.4 meters in the oceans' level. The main producers of CO2 are the private cars and the thermic centrals of electricity production.

Since 1860, humanity has spent more than ten times the energy it spent during the former one million years, using mostly fossil fuel, thus leading to a predictable depletion and end of petrol, gas, and uranium in the next decades.

Most essential minerals for modern industry and agriculture will be totally depleted before 2100.

Simultaneously, human population growth has already surpassed the planet's carrying capacity for food and other vital items, and the human population will not be able to keep expanding for much longer: The global food security index passed from 103 days in 1960 to 54 days in 1989, and to much less at present (Galhano Alves, 1994b; Ramade, 1989).

the breakdown of local and global ecosystems' homeostasis. Each year, the human populations of mostly techno-industrial urban societies consume twenty-five percent more natural resources than nature's productivity can create. The drastic rarefaction or end of natural resources is now a present and lasting possibility (Galhano Alves, 1994b), and may be an obstacle that the superstructure will not be able to surmount.

Moreover, as virtual money growth is now permanently in advance of the production growth of real merchandise, its value must be supported at every moment by a subsequent real production growth. Future resource exploitation and work are needed to justify present virtual growth. The superstructural race toward the *future* (as an *abstract future*) resulted in a situation in which time becomes out of phase from the present, being relocated into the future. The future growth of merchandise production is a requirement to support a present abstract increase of money. In this sense, present work and production growth are out of phase with present needs; they are already burned out in the future (thus such work is called *dead work*) to support present abstract money growth. Present money growth may never be supported by any type of productive work, generating a financial collapse in the exchange value of money.

Because natural resources cannot support present or future production intrinsic growth needs, and consumption begins to attain the limits of its spectacular effects, there will be a point at which merchandise and capital cannot grow anymore, causing the collapse of the whole structure. Moreover, the present status of living and mineral resources may not satisfy even the basic needs of the human population, and thus, the race toward the *future* may mean, presently or in a near future, a general involution of human living conditions. Violent social rebellions, violent repression by political powers, and

---

So, the global situation is catastrophic, leading humanity to a real collective suicide, that would be shared by the extinction of one half of the remaining living species and by the massive destruction of the ecosystems and natural habitats.

Also, presently, the nomadic and growing World war that exist since the end of World War II (1939-1945) increases and become a total growing war in many zones of the Planet, using weapons more and more technologically strongest, with much more *death power*.

great wars[1] will certainly accompany such processes, shaping, together

1. Through Human Pre-History and History, War didn't stop existing among humans. Its causes are multiples, and changed along the centuries and from culture to culture. Other primate species, like the chimpanzees, make also war between groups, but Humans are the only species that makes genocides, biocides and ecocides.

   2 081 years ago (from 2003), Rome, with its army commanded by the future Emperor Caius Julius Cesar, conquered Gaule (France, but also Belgium, Switzerland and many other territories) because of its important wine production, by simple territorial expansion, and also for the personal propaganda of Caius Julius Cesar among Romans and the conquered peoples, for him to become Emperor of Rome, leading alone all the huge Roman Empire, all around Mediterranean Sea *(Mare Nostrum* - "Our Sea" - for Romans) (César, 57-44 BC).

   During the XXth century, the two World' Wars were made by territorial, economic, ideology, and ethnic, racist, reasons.

   Wars began also for conquering natural resources, like, for instance, water. This is partially the case of the war from Israel against Palestine and Lebanon.

   In the XXIth century, the war is also made for food. For example, the war of Russian invasion of Ukraine, which began in February 2022, has as goals the Russian territorial expansion and security, and the control of an important part of cereals' World production and of other items. This status would give to Russia a global power by the control of food, not forgetting that Russia also has an important part of the World' exploitation of fuel, like the natural gas.

   Through the last decades, war has been also made by a fracture among civilizations, partially linked to the dark memories of the European Empires. Since the XVth century, those Empires created in the dominated nations (mostly in the Southern Hemisphere) a tendency to revanche the great sufferings and losses that existed all along the last 600 years (24 generations, if we consider that the space of time between generations is of 25 years).

   An immersion in these tragic histories generates a regain of proudness and recalls the founding ideas of these cultures, nations or countries.

   It is in this context that exists presently a total war made by radical religious groups, self-called Islamic, which goal is the destruction of the so-called western culture, and this by various methods. First creating terror in human populations, for them to become submitted, but also wining territorial power and sabotaging resources, as for instance the uranium mines in the North-East of Niger (francophone West Africa), taking in account the dependance of France on the Niger uranium, for nuclear power electricity production.

   This is the political and war game in countries like Mali and Niger, facing the guerrilla and razzia armed forces of Al Qaeda for the Islamic Maghreb.

   While, more in the South, in Nigeria and in the South-East of Niger, Boko Haram (which name means "the western education is bad") takes possession of petrol resources and of the dominated populations.

   These groups of totalitarian religious ideology have also the goal of conquering territories with a size of countries, to impose there their authoritarian regime, with any Human Right, based in a totalitarian and wrong interpretation of, for instance, the religious funding texts of these cultures, like the Coran, for example, among Muslims.

with natural catastrophes caused by human activities, an even more dangerous, inhospitable, and violent world than the present one. These factors configure a frontier that the superstructure may not be able to cross.

If production and capital growth stop, or, more probably, decreases to negative numbers (in economic terms; this is happening presently in several economic sectors), and this time in a real context determined by Nature and not just by financial imbalance, as it happened in the 1920s, we may ask what will happen to most humans, who live now in urban and virtual minimal biodiversity environments, in a state of total dependency? Probably, such artificial simulacrum systems will collapse, caused by a lack of basic resources such as food, water, energy, and rough materials. Urban populations will then face radical scarcity, and their survival will not be certain. As we saw, those populations are intrinsically dependent on work, money, and consumption, and no longer know how to survive by themselves. They will not have many alternatives other than fighting for survival and basic resources - a pointless fight in urban artificial and inert environments. Most probably, social violence, extreme scarcity, and the lack of alternative ways of living will cause an implosion of urban and techno-industrial superstructures.

Other modern political and social totalitarian forms exalt the foundation idea of the Nation, in a wrong and alienated way, like the idea of the "Great Russia", of Vladimir Vladimirovitch Putin and his entourage, during his absolutist reign, in the beginning of the XXIth century and of the IIIth millennium.

This justifies, in part, the Russian invasion war in Ukraine, started in February 2022, because the Moscow power consider it has making part of the "Great Russia", and does not accept its independence.

It was by the Ukraine and West Russia rivers that passed the Nordic Rus people, who build the first cities in their commercial route from the Great North till Constantinople (after called Istanbul). And the Rus are often considered has the ancestors of Russians.

Moreover, the absolute reign over an enormous territory, brings the Dictator egocentric and narcissist; he does anymore measure the ways to reach his unilateral goals, even in the spent of his own people, that he sees dying and suffering. He is also unable to take conscience that by this totalitarian power and by war, he compromises the place of his country in the World, and put it in risk of regression.

This is the destiny of all the great dictators, and of the peoples and countries that support them.

In the middle of the XXth century, Winston Churchill, British Prime Minister during the World War II, said that "*all the political regimes are bad, but the less bad of all is Democracy*".

One way to prevent and surmount such scenarios in the near future would be to invert the historical process that led to the formation of the present land property, production, and consumption systems, which in turn led to the huge mass migration toward urban centers. As we saw, land use and property systems are the basis of the historical processes that led to the present and near future situations.[1]

Maybe the ideal land use system is a combination of communitarian land use with small-scale family or individual private use. The latter allows each person to make his own choices and keep his own freedom from the community, if included in a context of common rights to land and resource use. The systems that I described in the beginning of this book are evidence of this. During the last few centuries, communitarian systems have generally been considered to be backward and primitive. However, such systems may allow resource management strategies compatibles with the conservation of biodiversity, natural resources, and ecological balances. Such systems may also ensure the potential of each person or human group to survive by themselves. Most probably, in case of global ecological and social collapse, the peoples who will survive and sustain a decent life will be those who maintain common land and resource systems, along with small-scale family agricultural and other productive activities, in total or high biodiversity ecosystems. Such people still know how to survive by themselves, independently of the global techno-industrial production and consumption system.

Will all humanity follow this course? The answer may be no, since all the political, social, and ecological conditions are not present. Today's peasant political movements are not fighting for restoration of communitarian land use, but for changes in private land distribution or for the control of agricultural production technologies and trade. That is the case of present peasants' fights in Brazil or in France (Bové & Dufour, 2000; Confédération Paysanne, 2002), which have global repercussions in the media and, in a smaller way, in agricultural policies.[2] However, excepting some "native peoples"

1. In this context, we must remember that, as Pierre Coulomb pointed out, "Every change in agricultural policies causes a 'crisis' that has deep effects on political systems; inversely, usually a change in political system causes a change in agricultural policy" (Coulomb, 1994).
2. Present alter-globalization peasant political movements fight mostly for "producing better and in other ways; creation of new peasant jobs; environment and natural resource conservation; and a ban on genetically modified organisms." Their strategy

political movements such as the Zapatista movement in Mexico, which are not representative of the global context, no political or social movement is presently fighting for a reform of land use and property systems toward a restoration of communitarian management and use of land. The "return to the land" movement of the 1960s and 1970s in Europe and America by small groups of people (Bison et al., 1994) had no significant impact either. Those movements are exceptions to the rule, without expression or parallel in national or global policies and tendencies. Urban social and political movements are also far removed from such goals. As in other techno-industrial mass consumption societies throughout the nineteenth and twentieth centuries, the inhabitants are more likely fighting for work, money, and consumption, or, what is the same, to maintain their present dependent condition. Identically, restoration of communitarian land uses is not in the agenda of any present government or international organization.

Moreover, it is presently unlikely that a mass migration from urban areas to rural and natural ones would solve the present and near future local and global problems. An inversion of the last centuries' migration processes would be possible if several conditions were to exist: (1) Common land should occupy most territory; (2) people should be able to survive on land and natural resources; and (3) the ecosystem's carrying capacity should be able to support such a migration. As we have seen, the two first conditions are nonexistent; it is possible to imagine social changes that would build them up, but in practical terms they are unachievable. Concerning the last condition, the fact is that the present global human population is more than 7.5 billion people, in a planet that (according to Ramade, 1989) has a carrying capacity of only 1.5 billion people (i.e., the global population in 1850). Thus, a massive migration from urban areas to rural or natural landscapes would just accelerate the present global ecological collapse, as it would cause the destruction of most natural habitats and of the few remaining local, balanced sociocultural systems of nature use.

Moreover, as I pointed out above, most ecosystems are already nearly destroyed. Only by massive reforestation could vegetation cover be restored, in areas progressively enlarged around those still

includes "an alliance among peasants, consumers, and ecologists" (Bové & Dufour, 2000). Despite their fight against property of organisms by capitalist multinational biochemical enterprises, they never mention land property rights.

balanced areas, allowing dispersal and expansion of the remaining wild fauna populations, but such actions have not been implemented yet, nor are there any such plans in the agenda of any present political organization.

As I mentioned before, Pierre Coulomb (1994) pointed out that, "In all the present industrialised countries, including the most recent ones (the new industrial countries of Asia) the establishment of a modern property right, the individual or private one, preceded (or has been concomitant with) the beginnings of industrialization." This historical process, with very ancient roots, is now coming, most probably, to an impasse, caused by the social, psychological, and ecological reasons pointed out in this book. Present techno-industrial mass production and consumption societies and their social and political superstructures are born from mass deprivation from free access to land and its natural resources. These societies were created, as I pointed out above, by the plunder and destruction of common territories and resources, in a bloody sequence of violence, terror, massacre, swindling and exploitation. Most probably, these simulacrum societies will end in the same way, leaving for the *future* a much poorer, violent, and more miserable planet than it once was.

As Freud (1930) wrote, "A real change in human beings' relationships with property would be much more helpful than any ethic orders." The communitarian systems of land use, together with small-scale family "private" systems, allowed the preservation of ecosystems and sustained humankind during most of its evolution. The maintenance of such systems among some present human groups and regions has a real political and ecological value for the present and future evolution of mankind and of all other species. But for most people, anxiety about the future is real, and it might be only a symptom of a sad reality that will not have a happy end (Galhano Alves, 2009, 2021, 2023).

References

Bernard, C. (1865). *Introduction à l'étude de la médecine expérimentale.* Paris (France) : (? p.)

Bison, E., Imarazene, R., Galhano Alves, J. P., Kraishi, K., & Alvar Bestilleiro, M. (1993). *Les néo-ruraux: Difficultés d'implantation en Ardèche.* In *Etude du milieu rural à l'échelle régionale : Le canton des Vans (Ardèche)—Rapport de Stage.* Montpellier, France : Institut Agronomique Méditerranéen de Montpellier/Centre International de Hautes Etudes Agronomiques Méditerranéennes (10 p.)

Bourbouse, A., & Rubino, R. (1992). *Terres collectives en Méditerranée : Histoire, législation, usages et modes d'utilisation par les animaux.* Villa d'Agri, Italia : Réseau F.A.O. Ovins et Caprins, Réseau Parcours Euro-Africain (279 p.)

Bové, J., & Dufour, F. (2000). *Le monde n'est pas une marchandise : Des paysans contre la malbouffe. Entretiens avec Gilles Luneau.* Paris, France : Editions La Découverte (239 p.)

Bowlby, J. (1973). *Apego e Perda: Vol. 1. El vínculo afectivo.* Barcelona, España (1993) : Ediciones Paidós Ibérica, S.A., Biblioteca de psicología profunda (418 p.)

Bowlby, J. (1973). *Apego e Perda: Vol. 3. Perda, tristeza e depressão.* São Paulo (Brasil) (1985) : Livraria Martins Fontes Editora Ltda. (486 p.)

Bühler, C. (1962). *A psicologia na vida do nosso tempo.* Lisboa, Portugal (1978) : Fundação Calouste Gulbenkian (632 p.)

Buonarotti. (1828). *L'histoire de la conspiration pour l'égalité dite de Babeuf.* Bruxelles, Belgique : (2 p.)

CÉSAR, C. J. (57-44 AC.). *La Guerre des Gaules (Commentarii de Bello Gallico)* - Rome, Italie, Empire romain / Paris, France : folio classique Gallimard (? p.)

Chartiot, A. (2003) - *Les rois de la Terre. Approche ethno-historique des relations entre les lions, les hommes et la sauvegarde de la nature.* Montpellier, France : Université de Lettres et de Sciences Sociales de

Montpellier/Paul Valéry (Université de Montpellier III) (Mémoire de Maîtrise) (116 p.)

Chollet, L. (2000). *L'insurrection situationniste.* Paris, France : Editions Dagorno (351 p.)

Confédération Paysanne (2002). *Changeons de politique agricole.* Paris, France : Editions Mille et une Nuits (144 p.)

Coulomb, P. (1994). *De la terre à l'état : Eléments pour un cours de politique agricole.* Montpellier, France : ENGREF, INRA-ESR Laboratoire d'Economie des Transitions (47 p.)

Darwin, C. (1859). *L'origine des espèces au moyen de la sélection naturelle ou la préservation des races favorisées dans la lutte pour la vie.* Paris, France (1992) : Flammarion (604 p.)

Debord, G. (1988). *Commentaires sur la société du spectacle, suivi de Préface à la quatrième édition italienne de "La société du spectacle".* Paris, France (1992) : Gallimard (113 p.)

Debord, G. (1967). *La société du spectacle.* Paris, France (1992) : Gallimard (169 p.)

DeGeorges, P. J., & Nochy, A. (undated). *Le loup, "affaire d'Etat."* Paris, France : http://carnivore library2.free.fr/proses_loup.pdf (35 p.)

Descola, P. (1986). *La nature domestique: Symbolisme et praxis dans l'écologie des Achuar.* Paris, France : Editions de la Maison des Sciences de l'Homme (450 p.)

Diakov, V. & Kovalev, S. (1973). *La société primitive.* Lisboa, Portugal : Editorial Estampa (120 p.)

Dias, J. (1984). *Rio de Onor: Comunitarismo agro-pastoril.* Lisboa, Portugal : Editorial Presença (353 p.)

Freud, S. (1930). *O mal-estar na civilização.* Rio de Janeiro, Brasil (1974) : Imago Editora (109 p.)

Friedman, G. (1963). *O futuro do trabalho humano.* São Paulo, Brasil (1968) : Moraes editores (272 p.)

GALHANO ALVES, J.P. (2023). *Coexistence des sociétés humaines et des écosystèmes. Les terres communautaires, leur élimination et ses conséquences* (préface de Farid Benhammou). Paris, France : Editions L'Harmattan (144 p.)

GALHANO ALVES, J. P. (2021). *O mundo de simulacro artificial. A eliminação geopolítica do uso comunitário da terra e os seus efeitos na nossa presente condição global* - Lisboa, Portugal & São Paulo, Brasil : Lisbon International Press (110 p.)

GALHANO ALVES, J. P. (2012). *Anthropologie et écosystèmes au Niger. Humains, lions et esprits de la forêt dans la culture gourmantché.* Paris, France : Éditions l'Harmattan (448 p.)

GALHANO ALVES, J.P. (2011). *Antropología e ecosistemas. Vivir en biodiversidad total con leones, tigres o lobos. India – Niger – Portugal* (presentación de Fernando Palacios. Prefacios de Amélia Frazão Moreira y de Danièle Vazeilles). Madrid, España : Gobierno de España; Ministerio de Ciencia e Innovación de España; Ministerio de Medio Ambiente y Medio Rural y Marino de España; Museo Nacional de Ciencias Naturales de España; Consejo Superior de Investigaciones Científicas de España; Año Internacional de la Diversidad Biológica 2010 de la ONU/UN; Fondo Europeo Agrícola de Desarrollo Rural (FEADER), Unión Europea (168 p.)

GALHANO ALVES, J.P. (2009a). *The artificial simulacrum world. The geopolitical elimination of communitary land use and its effects on our present global condition*. New York, NY, USA : Eloquent Books (71 p.).

GALHANO ALVES, J.P. (2009 b). *Viver com leões. A coexistência entre humanos e biodiversidade no W do Níger. Os Gourmantché*. Porto, Portugal : Trabalhos de Antropologia e Etnologia, Sociedade Portuguesa de Antropologia e de Etnologia, Vol. 49 (1-4). (pp. 57-77)

GALHANO ALVES, J.P. (2009c). *From land to a simulacrum world; an anthropological essay on the history of an agricultural geo-policy: the elimination of communitary land use systems and its ecological, socio-cultural, psychological and political effects*. Bloomington, Indiana, USA : The Digital Library of the Commons, Indiana University (31 p.)

GALHANO ALVES, J.P. (2008). *Living with lions*. New Delhi, India : Down To Earth, Centre for Science and Environment, Vol. 17, nº 6, August 1-15, 2008 (pp. 48-50)

Galhano Alves, J. P. (2007a). *Caçar com os 'génios:' Representações da natureza e conservação da biodiversidade no Parque Nacional do W, Niger*. Porto, Portugal : Trabalhos de Antropologia e Etnologia, Vol. 47 (1-4) (pp. 93-122)

Galhano Alves, J. P. (2007b). *Human societies and lions in W National Park region (Niger). A synopsis of lion related matters developed in an anthropology of nature research.* Brandhof, South Africa : African Lion News: Official newsletter of the African Lion Working Group, IUCN, Species Survival Commission, Cat and Conservation Breeding Specialist Group, Vol. 7 (pp. 27-44)

GALHANO ALVES, J. P. (2003). *Des hommes, des grands carnivores et des grands herbivores. Une approche anthropologique et comparative international.* Porto, Portugal : Antropológicas, nº7, CEAA Centro de Estudos de Antropologia Aplicada, Edições Universidade Fernando Pessoa (pp. 75-114)

Galhano Alves, J. P. (2002). *Vivre en biodiversité totale : Des hommes, des grands carnivores et des grands herbivores sauvages. Deux études de cas : loups au Portugal, tigres en Inde*. Lille, France : Atelier National de Reproduction des Thèses (880 p.)

GALHANO ALVES, J. P. (2000). *Vivre en biodiversité totale. Des hommes, des grands carnivores et des grands herbivores sauvages. Deux études de cas : loups au Portugal, tigres en Inde*. Aix-en-Provence, France : Doctorate Thesis in Anthropology - Laboratoire d'Ecologie Humaine et d'Anthropologie, UMR 6591 du Centre National de Recherche Scientifique (CNRS), Université de Droit, d'Economie et des Sciences d'Aix-Marseille (Université d'Aix-Marseille III) (880 p.)

Galhano Alves, J. P. (1999). *Men and tigers in Sariska Tiger Reserve, India*. Bougy, Switzerland : Cat News, Newsletter of the Cat Specialist Group, Species Survival Commission, International Union for the Conservation of Nature (IUCN), No. 30 (pp. 10-12).

Galhano Alves, J. P. (1995). *Etude des rapports synergiques entre des sociétés rurales et leur environnement en état de totale biodiversité: L'exemple de la vallée de Sariska (Rajasthan, Inde)—Intégration entre sociétés rurales, grands herbivores et grands prédateurs* (Master of Science Thesis). Montpellier, France : Institut Agronomique Méditerranéen de Montpellier/ Centre International de Hautes Etudes Agronomiques Méditerranéennes (543 p.)

Galhano Alves, J. P. (1994a). *Le rapport et l'équilibre possible entre les sociétés rurales et l'environnement minéral et vivant. Propositions pour une étude générale et une étude de cas : Sociétés rurales, grands herbivores et super-prédateurs de la vallée de Sariska, Rajasthan, Inde*. Montpellier, France: Institut Agronomique Méditerranéen de Montpellier/Centre International de Hautes Etudes Agronomiques Méditerranéennes (Mémoire de DSPU) (63 p.)

Galhano Alves, J. P. (1994b). *Les baldios*. In *Politiques Foncières et Aménagements des Structures Agricoles dans les Pays Méditerranéens. Communications*. Montpellier, France : Çukurova University, Turkey & Centre International de Hautes Etudes Agronomiques Méditerranéennes/ Institut Agronomique Méditerranéen de Montpellier, France (15 p.)

Galhano Alves, J. P., & Garcia-Perea, R. (1998). *Tigers and people: Strategies for tiger conservation in Sariska Tiger Reserve, India*. Bougy, Switzerland : Cat News, Newsletter of the Cat Specialist Group, Species Survival Commission, International Union for the Conservation of Nature (IUCN), No. 29 (pp. 9-11)

Heinrich, D., & Hergt, M. (1993). *Atlas de l'Écologie*. Paris, France : Le Livre de Poche (286 p.)

Kovaliov, S. I. (1948). *Historia de Roma*. Madrid, España (1992) : Ediciones Akal (874 p.)

Krisis (Förderverein) (1999). *Manifest gegen die arbeit*. Berlin, Deutschland : Zeitschrift Krisis (79 p.)

Kundera, M. (1983). *A insustentável leveza do ser*. Lisboa, Portugal (1986) : Publicações Dom Quixote (364 p.).

Landauer, T. K. (1972). *Psicología*. Cali, Colombia : Libros McGraw-Hill de Mexico (382 p.)

La Sainte Bible (1966). Valence, France : Bibles et publications chrétiennes (296 p.)

Lenine, V. I. U. (1923). *Sobre a cooperação*. In Marx et al. (1974), *Cooperativismo e socialismo*. Coimbra: Portugal : Centelha (pp. 35-47)

Leroi-Gourhan, A. (1965). *O gesto e a palavra: Vol. 2. Memória e ritmos*. Lisboa, Portugal (1983) : Edições 70 (247 p.).

Lopez, B. H. (1978). *Of wolves and men*. New York, USA : Charles Scribner's Sons (309 p.)

Marcuse, H. (1976). *Un nouvel ordre*. In Manière de voir (2001), *Sociétés sous contrôle*. Paris, France : Le Monde Diplomatique, No. 56 (pp. 10-12)

Martí, O. (2007). *Un nuevo grito de guerra en Francia: "No a 2007"*. Madrid, España : El País, 2 January 2007, (p. 7)

Marx, K. (1883). *Le capital* (résumé par Gabriel Deville). Paris, France : C. Marpon et E. Flammarion (324 p.)

Marx, K. (1872). *Da manufactura à fábrica automática*. In Marglin et al. (1974), *Divisão social do trabalho, ciência, técnica e modo de produção capitalista*. Porto, Portugal : Publicações Escorpião (pp. 235-252)

Plato (399 - 390 BC). *Protagoras* (traduit par Frédérique Ildefonse). Paris, France (1997) : Flammarion (266 p.)

Powell, T. G. E. (1958). *Os celtas*. Lisboa, Portugal (1965) : Editorial Verbo (282 p.)

Ramade, F. (1989). *Eléments d'écologie : Ecologie appliquée*. Paris, France : MacGraw-Hill (578 p.)

Ribeiro, S., Cristóvão, A., & Galhano, J. (2004). *Communal land use and management systems in Northern Portugal*. In *(Pre)Proceedings of the Sixth European IFSA Symposium: Vol. 2 (4–7 April 2004). European farming and society in search of a new social contract. Learn to manage change. Farming and rural systems research and extension*. Vila Real, Portugal : International Farming Systems Association; Universidade de Trás-os-Montes e Alto Douro (pp. 923-924)

Rodrigues, M. (1987). *Os baldios*. Lisboa, Portugal: Editorial Caminho (? p.).

Rowell, T. E. (1967). *La variabilité de l'organisation sociale des primates*. In Morris, D., *L'éthologie des primates*. Bruxelles, Belgique : Editions Complexe (pp. 242-261)

Seattle, N. (1854). Quoted in *Por fim talvez sejamos irmãos*. Lisboa, Portugal (1977) : Comissão Nacional do Ambiente (32 p.)

Sopeña, G. (2002). *Mucho más que rudos guerreros : El mundo celta*. Madrid, España : GEO, G y J España Ediciones, no. 186 (pp.78-82)

Thapar, V. (undated). *The cult of the tiger (Report for Project Tiger)*. New Delhi, India : Ministry of Environment and Forests (68 p.)

Torri, M. C. (2005). *La conservation et l'utilisation durable des ressources naturelles et la gestion participative. Le cas de la région de la Réserve Naturelle de Tigres de Sariska (Rajasthan, Inde)* (Master of Science Thesis). Montpellier, France : Série Master of Science, No. 72, Centre International de Hautes Etudes Agronomiques Méditerranéennes / Institut Agronomique Méditerranéen de Montpellier (215 p.)

Tse-Tung, M. (1969). *Sobre a justa solução das contradições no seio do povo*. Porto, Portugal (1974) : Edições do Povo (94 p.).

Vaneigem, R. (1999). *Pour une internationale du genre humain*. Paris, France : Le cherche midi éditeur (183 p.)

OTHER PUBLICATIONS OF THE AUTHOR, João Pedro GALHANO ALVES

BOOKS

Galhano Alves, J.P. (2023). "Coexistence des sociétés humaines et des écosystèmes. Les terres communautaires, leur élimination et ses conséquences" (préface de Farid Benhammou) - Editions L'Harmattan - Paris, France - 144 p.

Galhano Alves, J.P. (2021). "O mundo de simulacro artificial. A eliminação geopolítica do uso comunitário da terra e os seus efeitos na nossa presente condição global" - Lisbon International Press - Lisboa, Portugal & São Paulo, Brasil - 110 p.

Galhano Alves, J.P. (2012). "Anthropologie et écosystèmes au Niger. Humains, lions et esprits de la forêt dans la culture gourmantché " - Éditions L'Harmattan - Paris, France - 448 p.

Galhano Alves, J.P. (2011). "Antropología y ecosistemas. Vivir en biodiversidad total con leones, tigres o lobos. India – Niger - Portugal" (Presentación de Fernando Palacios. Prefacios de Amélia Frazão Moreira y Danièle Vazeilles) - Gobierno de España; Ministerio de Ciencia y Innovación de España; Ministerio de Medio Ambiente y Medio Rural y Marino de España; Museo Nacional de Ciencias Naturales de España; Consejo Superior de Investigaciones Científicas de España; Año Internacional de la Diversidad Biológica 2010 de la ONU/UN; Fondo Europeo Agrícola de Desarrollo Rural (FEADER), Unión Europea – Madrid, España - 168 p.

Galhano Alves, J.P. (2009). "The artificial simulacrum world. The geopolitical elimination of communitary land use and its effects on our present global condition" – Eloquent Books – New York, NY, USA – 71 p.

Riego Celada, Luís del; Galhano Alves, J.P. (prefacio de Ramón Grande del Brío). (2006). "Recorrido por los relatos loberos de Sanabria y Tras os Montes; edición bilingüe castellano y portugués" - [Incl. - Galhano Alves,

J.P. "Algunos ejemplos de relatos, opiniones, tradiciones orales u prácticas relacionadas con el lobo en la región del Parque Natural de Montesinho (Tras-os-Montes). Corto epítome etnográfico", pp. 22-30. / "Alguns exemplos de relatos, opiniões, tradições orais ou práticas relacionadas com o lobo na região do Parque Natural de Montesinho (Trás-os-Montes). Curta epítome etnográfica", pp. 51-59] - Ayuntamiento de Puebla de Sanabria ; Junta de Castilla y León; Gabinete de Iniciativas Transfronterizas; Feder Unión Europea - Puebla de Sanabria, España - 60 p.

Galhano Alves, J.P. (2002). "Vivre en Biodiversité Totale. Des hommes, des grands carnivores et des grands herbivores sauvages. Deux études de cas : loups au Portugal, tigres en Inde" (deux tomes) (Thèse de Doctorat de 2000, publiée) – Collection Thèse à la Carte, Presses universitaires du Septentrion / Atelier National de Reproduction des Thèses (ANRT) – Villeneuve d'Ascq, France - 880 p.

THESIS

Galhano Alves, J.P. (2000). "Vivre en biodiversité totale. Des hommes, des grands carnivores et des grands herbivores sauvages. Deux études de cas: loups au Portugal, tigres en Inde" - Thèse de Doctorat en Anthropologie - Laboratoire d'Écologie Humaine et d'Anthropologie, UMR 6591 du Centre National de Recherche Scientifique (CNRS), Université de Droit, d'Economie et des Sciences d'Aix-Marseille (Université d'Aix-Marseille III) - Aix-en-Provence, France - 880 p.

Galhano Alves, J.P. (1995). "Étude des rapports synergiques entre des sociétés rurales et leur environnement en état de totale biodiversité. L'exemple de la vallée de Sariska (Rajasthan, Inde) : intégration entre sociétés rurales, grands herbivores et grands prédateurs" - Thèse de Master of Science de Hautes Études en Politiques Agricoles et Administration du Développement - Centre International de Hautes Etudes Agronomiques Méditerranéennes / Institut Agronomique Méditerranéen de Montpellier - Montpellier, France - 543 p.

MEMORIES

Galhano Alves, J.P. (1994). "Le rapport et l'équilibre possible entre les sociétés rurales et l'environnement minéral et vivant. Propositions pour une étude générale et une étude de cas : sociétés rurales, grands herbivores et super-prédateurs de la vallée de Sariska, Rajasthan, Inde" - Mémoire de Diplôme de Spécialisation Post-Universitaire – DSPU - en Développement Rural / Projet de thèse de Master of Science de Hautes Études - Centre International de Hautes Etudes Agronomiques Méditerranéennes / Institut Agronomique Méditerranéen de Montpellier - Montpellier, France - 63 p.

Galhano Alves, J.P. (1987). "O trabalho infantil na agricultura. Uma primeira aproximação" - Relatório de Estágio de Investigação em Sociologia Rural,

Licenciatura em Engenharia Agrícola (Agronomia) - Universidade de Trás-os-Montes e Alto Douro - Vila Real, Portugal - 161 p.

SCIENTIFIC ARTICLES

Articles published in scientific reviews with reading comitee

Galhano Alves, J.P. (2009). "Viver com leões. A coexistência entre humanos e biodiversidade no W do Níger. Os Gourmantché" – Trabalhos de Antropologia e Etnologia, Sociedade Portuguesa de Antropologia e de Etnologia, Vol. 49 (1-4) – Porto, Portugal – pp. 57-77.

Galhano Alves, J.P. (2009). "From land to a simulacrum world; an anthropological essay on the history of an agricultural geo-policy: the elimination of communitary land use systems and its ecological, socio-cultural, psychological and political effects" – The Digital Library of the Commons, Indiana University – Bloomington, Indiana, USA – 31 p.

Galhano-Alves, J.P. (2008). "Living with lions" – Down To Earth, Centre for Science and Environment, Vol. 17, nº 6, August 1-15, 2008 – New Delhi, India - pp. 48-50.

Galhano-Alves, J.P. (2007). "Caçar com os "génios". Representações da natureza e conservação da biodiversidade no Parque Nacional do W, Niger" – Trabalhos de Antropologia e Etnologia, Sociedade Portuguesa de Antropologia e de Etnologia, Vol. 47 (1-4) – Porto, Portugal – pp. 93-122.

Blanco, Juan Carlos; Galhano Alves, J.P.; Englebert, Florence. (2007). "Les grands prédateurs à Travers l'Europe – Péninsule Ibérique" - La Voie du Loup, nº27, Mission Loup de FNE, France Nature Environnement, Fédération Française des Associations de Protection de la Nature et de l'Environnement – Paris, France - pp. 12-14.

Galhano-Alves, J.P. (2007). "Human societies and lions in W National Park region (Niger). A synopsis of lion related matters developed in an anthropology of nature research" - African Lion News, Vol. 7 (April 2007), Official newsletter of the African Lion Working Group, IUCN, Species Survival Commission, Cat and Conservation Breeding Specialist Group - Brandhof, South Africa – pp. 27-44.

Galhano-Alves, J.P. (2004). "Men and wild Boar. A study in Montesinho Natural Park (Portugal)" - Wild Boar Research 2002. A selection of edited papers from the 4th International Wild Boar Symposium. Galemys, The Spanish Mammal Journal, vol. 16 (N.E.), Sociedad Española para la Conservación y Estudio de los Mamíferos SECEM - Málaga, España - pp. 223-230.

Galhano Alves, J.P. (2004). – "Restaurer et coexister avec la biodiversité totale. Sociétés humaines, grands carnivores et grands herbivores sauvages. Une approche multidisciplinaire et comparative internationale». Recherches naturalistes en région Centre, nº 14, décembre 2004, Nature Centre, Conservatoire du patrimoine naturel de la région centre - Orléans, France - pp. 141-148.

Galhano Alves, J.P. (2003). "Des hommes, des grands carnivores et des grands herbivores. Une approche anthropologique et comparative internationale" - Antropológicas, nº7, CEAA Centro de Estudos de Antropologia Aplicada, Edições Universidade Fernando Pessoa - Porto, Portugal - pp. 75-114.

Galhano Alves, J.P. (2002). "Tigers, wolves & biodiversity" - Wolf Print, issue 13, summer 2002, The UK Wolf Conservation Trust - Reading, England - pp. 9-13.

Galhano Alves, J.P. (2000). "Du tigre au loup : la biodiversité totale est l'avenir de l'homme" - La Voie du Loup, nº 7, Mission Loup, France Nature Environnement (Fédération Française des Associations de Protection de la Nature et de l'Environnement) - Paris, France - pp. 18-21.

Galhano Alves, J.P. (1999). "Of large Carnivores and humans" - Down to Earth, vol. 8, nº 4, July 15, Centre for Science and Environment - New Delhi, India - pp. 27-31.

Galhano Alves, J.P. (1999). "Men and tigers in Sariska Tiger Reserve, India" - Cat News, nº 30, Newsletter of the Cat Specialist Group, Species Survival Commission, International Union for the Conservation of Nature (IUCN) - Bougy, Switzerland - pp. 10-12.

Galhano Alves, J.P. and Garcia-Perea, R. (1998). " Tigers and people: strategies for tiger conservation in Sariska Tiger Reserve, India" - Cat News, nº 29, Newsletter of the Cat Specialist Group, Species Survival Commission, International Union for the Conservation of Nature (IUCN) - Bougy, Switzerland - pp. 9-11.

Galhano Alves, J.P. (1996). "A perfect world" - Down to Earth, vol. 5, nº 11, October 31, Centre for Science and Environment - New Delhi, India - pp. 32-34.

Articles published in other scientific reviews of international difusion

Galhano Alves, J.P. (2002). "Sociedades humanas y tigres. Desarrollo sostenible y restauración de la biodiversidad" (publicado conjuntamente con entrevistas personales en artículo anejo) - La Tierra, Publicación medioambiental SL, nº 50, Verano 2002 - Madrid, España - p. 60.

Artiles published in the Medias

Galhano Alves, J.P. (2008). "Social rules about dealing with lions in Niger" – The New Nation, Bangladesh's Independent News Source, August 18 2008 – Dhaka, Bangladesh – 1 p.

Galhano Alves, J.P. (1998). "Da conservação de lobos, tigres e outros grandes carnívoros. Algumas perguntas e respostas" - Além-Parte, Revista de cultura popular e opinión, nº 0 - Chantada, España - pp. 14-15.

ARTICLES IN SCIENTIFIC CONGRESSES BOOKS

Galhano Alves, J.P. (2008). "From land to a simulacrum world; An anthropological essay on the history of an agricultural geo-policy: the elimination of communitary land use systems and its ecological, socio-cultural, psychological and political effects" – 12th Biennial Conference of the International Association for the Study of the Commons, "Governing Sharing Resources: Connecting Local Experience to Global Challenges" - 14-18 July 2008 – Cheltenham, England – 31 p.

Galhano Alves, J.P. (2006). "Coexistence among Human and Lion Societies; a short outline of an ethnobiology research carried out in W National Park region (Niger)" - Xth International Congress of Ethnobiology (ICE 2006). Ethnobiology: Food, Health, and Cultural Landscape - 5-9 November 2006 - Contributions, Received Papers - The International Society of Ethnobiology; Thai Library Association; Khon Kaen University; Chiang Mai University; Rajabhat Chiang Rai University; Mae Fah Luang University - Chiang Rai, Thailand - 8 p.

Galhano Alves, J.P. (2006). " Bow and Arrow Hunting as Key Component of West Africa Savannah Societies' Use and Perceptions of Nature; the example of W National Park region, Niger" - Xth International Congress of Ethnobiology (ICE 2006). Ethnobiology: Food, Health, and Cultural Landscape - 5-9 November 2006 - Contributions, Received Papers - The International Society of Ethnobiology; Thai Library Association; Khon Kaen University; Chiang Mai University; Rajabhat Chiang Rai University; Mae Fah Luang University - Chiang Rai, Thailand - 4 p.

Ribeiro, Sónia; Cristóvão, Artur; Galhano, João. (2004). "Communal Land Use and Management Systems in Northern Portugal" - (Pre)Proceedings of the Sixth European IFSA Symposium. European farming and society in search of a new social contract. Learn to manage change. Farming and rural systems research and extension - 4-7 April 2004, Vol. II - International Farming Systems Association; Universidade de Trás-os-Montes e Alto Douro - Vila Real, Portugal - pp. 923-924.

Galhano Alves, J.P. (2003). "A Restauração da Biodiversidade Total e o Desenvolvimento Sustentável. Novos conceitos para a investigação e para a acção" - Actas do 2º Congresso Nacional de Conservação da Natureza, conservação e utilização sustentável da diversidade biológica - 2-5 Outubro 2001 - Instituto da Conservação da Natureza ; Ministério do Ambiente e do Ordenamento do Território; Fundação Calouste Gulbenkian - Lisboa, Portugal - 7 p.

Galhano Alves, J.P. (2001). "Conservar e Restaurar a Biodiversidade Total. Uma função estratégica dos espaços rurais" - IV Coloquio Hispano Portugués de Estudios Rurales - 7-8 junio 2001. Comunicaciones - Asociación Española de Economia Agraria; Instituto Universitario de Estudios e Desenvolvemento de Galicia IDEGA; Sociedade Portuguesa de Estudos Rurais; Universidad de Santiago de Compostela - Santiago de Compostela, España - 21 p.

ABSTRACTS AND TITLES PUBLISHED FOR CONTRIBUTIONS TO SCIENTIFIC CONGRESSES

Galhano Alves, J.P. (2012). "Humans, lions and biodiversity in the W of Niger. The Gourmantché culture" - "Bajo el Árbol de la Palabra: Resistencias y Transformaciones entre lo Local y lo Global", Libro del Congreso, 8º Congreso Ibérico de Estudios Africanos (CIEA 8), Grupo de Estudios Africanos (GEA), Facultad de Derecho, Universidad Autónoma de Madrid, 14-16 Junio 2012 – Madrid, España – pp. 269-270.

Galhano Alves, J.P. (2012). "Gourmantché religion and philosophy. Speaking with the "spiritual beings" of nature'. A study in Niger W region" - "Bajo el Árbol de la Palabra: Resistencias y Transformaciones entre lo Local y lo Global", Libro del Congreso, 8º Congreso Ibérico de Estudios Africanos (CIEA 8), Grupo de Estudios Africanos (GEA), Facultad de Derecho, Universidad Autónoma de Madrid, 14-16 Junio 2012 – Madrid, España – pp. 270-271.

Galhano Alves, J.P. & Wali, Soumaïla Mordia (2011). "Coexistence among humans, lions and biodiversity in the W of Niger" - "People makes places. Ways of feeling the wolrd", The 10th congress of the International Society of Ethnology and Folklore (SIEF), Faculdade de Ciências Sociais e Humanas, Universidade Nova de Lisboa, Panel 315, "Conflicts and perceptions of environment in Natural Protected Areas" – 17-21 April 2011 – Lisboa, Portugal – p. 248.

Galhano Alves, J.P. (2009). "Viver com leões. A coexistência entre humanos e biodiversidade no W do Níger. Os Gourmantché" - Livro do IV Congresso da Associação Portuguesa de Antropologia, Classificar o Mundo – 9-11 Setembro 2009 – Associação Portuguesa de Antropologia – Lisboa, Portugal – p. 251.

Galhano Alves, J.P. (2009). "Viver com leões. A coexistência entre humanos e biodiversidade no W do Níger. Os Gourmantché" - Programa do IV Congresso da Associação Portuguesa de Antropologia, Classificar o Mundo – 9-11 Setembro 2009 – Associação Portuguesa de Antropologia – Lisboa, Portugal – p. 45.

Galhano Alves, J.P. (2006). "Coexistence among Human and Lion Societies; a short outline of an ethnobiology research carried out in W National Park region (Niger)" - Program, Abstracts, and List of Participants. Xth International Congress of Ethnobiology, ICE 2006. Ethnobiology: Food, Health, and Cultural Landscape - 5-9 November 2006 - The International Society of Ethnobiology; Thai Library Association; Khon Kaen University; Chiang Mai University; Rajabhat Chiang Rai University; Mae Fah Luang University - Chiang Rai, Thailand - 8 p.

Galhano Alves, J.P. (2006). " Bow and Arrow Hunting as Key Component of West Africa Savannah Societies' Use and Perceptions of Nature; the example of W National Park region, Niger" - Program, Abstracts, and List of Participants. Xth International Congress of Ethnobiology, ICE 2006. Ethnobiology: Food, Health, and Cultural Landscape - 5-9 November 2006 - The International Society of Ethnobiology; Thai Library Association; Khon Kaen University; Chiang Mai University; Rajabhat Chiang Rai University; Mae Fah Luang University - Chiang Rai, Thailand - pp. 9-12.

Galhano Alves, J.P. (2006). "Uso e representações da natureza na região do Parque Nacional do W, Niger. Ilustrações a partir da caça com arco e outras práticas" - Terceiro Congresso da Associação Portuguesa de Antropologia. Afinidade e Diferença - 6-8 Abril 2006 - Resumos - Associação Portuguesa de Antropologia; Instituto de Ciências Sociais da Universidade de Lisboa; Instituto Superior de Ciências do Trabalho e da Empresa - Lisboa, Portugal - p. 22.

Galhano Alves, J.P. (2004). "Les rapports entre sociétés humaines, grands carnivores et biodiversité (tigre, lion, loup...)" - Colloque pluridisciplinaire de jeunes chercheurs et praticiens de terrain (Alpes - Pyrénées). La cohabitation avec les grands prédateurs en France (loup et ours). Enjeux didactiques pour la conservation de la nature et le développement durable - 21-22 mars 2004 - Le programme - Muséum des Sciences Naturelles d'Orléans ; ENGREF École Nationale du Génie Rural des Eaux et des Forêts (Paris) ; Institut de Recherches pour le Développement IRD d'Orléans ; Association des Géographes de l'Université d'Orléans ; FERUS ours-loup-lynx - Orléans, France - p. 2.

Galhano Alves, J.P. (2002). "Men and Wild Boar. A Study in Montesinho Natural Park (Portugal)" - 4th International Wild Boar Symposium - 19-22 September 2002 - Livro de abstracts - International Wild Boar Conservation Association ; Universidade de Aveiro - Lousã, Portugal - p. 9.

Galhano Alves, J.P. (2001). "A Restauração da Biodiversidade Total e o Desenvolvimento Sustentável. Novos Conceitos para a Investigação e para a Acção". "2º Congresso Nacional de Conservação da Natureza, conservação e utilização sustentável da diversidade biológica - 2-5 Outubro 2001 - Resumos - Instituto da Conservação da Natureza ; Ministério do Ambiente e do Ordenamento do Território; Fundação Calouste Gulbenkian - Lisboa, Portugal - p. 86.

Galhano Alves, J.P. (2001). " The Relationships between Humans and Wolves in the Montesinho Natural Park (North-east of Portugal): from Destruction to Conservation" - Canid Biology and Conservation International Conference - 17-21 September 2001 - Programme and abstracts - The Wildlife Conservation Research Unit of Oxford University; IUCN/SSC Canid Specialist Group - Oxford, England - p. 56.

Montserrat, Soria & Galhano Alves, J.P. (2001). " Analysis of Human Attitudes for Wolf Conservation: the case of Sierra de la Culebra (Spain)" - Canid Biology and Conservation International Conference - 17-21 September 2001 - Programme and abstracts - The Wildlife Conservation Research

Unit of Oxford University; IUCN/SSC Canid Specialist Group - Oxford, England - p. 104.

Galhano Alves, J.P. (2001). " Of Men, Large Carnivores and Large Wild Herbivores: a possible and necessary coexistence " - 8th International Theriological Congress - 12-17 August 2001 - Scientific programme and abstracts - The American Society of Mammalogists, International Theriological Commitee, Wildlife Group of the South African Veterinary Association, The British Council - Sun City, South Africa - p. 9.

Torri, Maria Costanza & Galhano Alves, J.P. (2001). "People's Participation for Tiger Conservation in Sariska Tiger Reserve, Rajasthan, India" - 8th International Theriological Congress - 12-17 August 2001 - Scientific programme and abstracts - The American Society of Mammalogists; International Theriological Committee; Wildlife Group of the South African Veterinary Association; The British Council - Sun City, South Africa - p. 19.

Galhano Alves, J.P. (2001). "Conservar e Restaurar a Biodiversidade Total. Uma função estratégica dos espaços rurais" - IV Coloquio Hispano Portugués de Estudios Rurales - 7-8 junio 2001 - Comunicaciones - Asociación Española de Economia Agraria; Instituto Universitario de Estudios e Desenvolvemento de Galicia IDEGA; Sociedade Portuguesa de Estudos Rurais; Universidad de Santiago de Compostela - Santiago de Compostela, España - 21 p.

Galhano Alves, J.P. (2001). "Conservar y Restaurar la Biodiversidad Total. Sociedades rurales, grandes carnívoros y grandes herbívoros salvajes. Dos estudios de caso: Lobos en Portugal, Tigres en la India" - I Jornadas Ibéricas de Ecologia da Paisagem - 17-21 Abril 2001 - Resumos - Escola Superior Agrária; Instituto Politécnico de Bragança; Departamento Interuniversitario de Ecología, Universidad de Alcalá; Associação Portuguesa de Ecologia da Paisagem; Asociación Española de Ecología Terrestre - Bragança, Portugal - p. 18.

Galhano Alves, J.P. (2001). "Sociedades Humanas, Lobos e Grandes Herbívoros Selvagens. Um ecossistema humanizado em estado de alta biodiversidade. O caso da região do Parque Natural de Montesinho (nordeste de Portugal)" - II Simpósio Internacional sobre Fauna Selvagem - 18-21 Abril 2001 - Livro de Abstracts - Universidade de Trás-os-Montes e Alto Douro ; WAVES - Vila Real, Portugal - p. 8.

Galhano Alves, J.P. (2001). "Sociedades Humanas, Tigres e Grandes Herbívoros Selvagens. Um ecossistema humanizado em estado de total biodiversidade. O caso da região da Reserva de Tigres de Sariska (Rajasthan, Índia)" - II Simpósio Internacional sobre Fauna Selvagem - 18-21 Abril 2001 - Livro de Abstracts - Universidade de Trás-os-Montes e Alto Douro ; WAVES - Vila Real, Portugal - p. 9.

Galhano Alves, J.P. (2001). "Conservar e Restaurar a Biodiversidade Total. Sociedades humanas, grandes carnívoros e grandes herbívoros selvagens" -

II Simpósio Internacional sobre Fauna Selvagem - 18-21 Abril 2001 - Livro de Abstracts - Universidade de Trás-os-Montes e Alto Douro ; WAVES - Vila Real, Portugal - p. 10.

Galhano Alves, J.P. (1999). "Sociedades Rurais, Lobos e Grandes Herbívoros no Parque Natural de Montesinho (Nordeste de Portugal)" - Congreso sobre la Recuperación del Lobo en Sierra Morena - 10-12 diciembre 1999 - Programa y Resúmenes - Diputación de Sevilla; Grupo Ecologista CICONIA; Universidad de Córdoba (Dpto. de Biología Animal) ; Federación de Espacios Naturales Protegidos de Andalucía; Asociación de Amigos de Doñana - Sevilla, España - pp. 45-46.

Galhano Alves, J.P. (1999). "Of Large Carnivores and Men. Two different realities: rural societies and tigers in the Sariska Tiger Reserve (Rajasthan, India); rural societies and wolves in the Montesinho Natural Park (north-east of Portugal)" - 2nd International Wildlife Management Congress - Wildlife, land and people: priorities for the 21st century - Program and abstracts - Gödöllõ, Hungary - p. 60.

TEXTS PUBLISHED FOR UNIVERSITARY COURSES

Galhano Alves, J.P. (2013). "Antropologia, civilizações e ecossistemas. Povos que vivem em biodiversidade total com leões, tigres ou lobos. Níger – Índia – Portugal" - Web-Site da Universidade do Porto, Centro de Estudos Africanos da Universidade do Porto, Universidade do Porto – Porto, Portugal – 30 p.

Galhano Alves, J.P. (2013). "Antropologia, civilizações e ecossistemas. Povos que vivem em biodiversidade total com leões, tigres ou lobos. Níger – Índia – Portugal" - Web-Site da Universidade Católica Portuguesa, Campus da Foz – Porto, Portugal – 30 p.

Galhano Alves, J.P. (2009). "Antropologia e ecossistemas. Viver em biodiversidade total com leões, tigres ou lobos. Níger – Índia – Portugal" – Conference sinopsis to the students and researchers, Escola Superior de Educação Jean Piaget, Instituto Piaget – Arcozelo, Vila Nova de Gaia, Portugal – 16 p.

Galhano Alves, J.P. (2009). "Anthropologie et écosystèmes. Vivre en biodiversité totale avec des lions, tigres ou loups. Niger – Inde – Portugal" – Conference sinopsis to the students and researchers, Faculté de Lettres et de Sciences Humaines, Université Abdou Moumouni (Université de Niamey) – Niamey, Niger - 14 p.

Galhano Alves, J.P. (2008). "Antropologia e ecossistemas. Viver em biodiversidade total com leões, tigres ou lobos. Níger, Índia, Portugal" – Conference sinopsis to the students and researchers, Mestrado em Antropologia Social e Cultural, Faculdade de Ciências e Tecnologia, Universidade de Coimbra - Coimbra, Portugal - 23 p.

Galhano Alves, J.P. (2006). " Uma geopolítica agrária: eliminação dos sistemas comunitários de uso da terra e suas implicações ecológicas, socio-culturais, psicológicas e políticas. Uma abordagem antropológica estrutural" - Conference sinopsis to the students and researchers, Mestrado Ibérico em Design e Produção Gráfica, Intermédia - 3ª edição, Universitat de Barcelona; Alquimia da Côr - Porto, Portugal - 23 p.

Galhano Alves, J.P. (2005). "Biodiversidad total y desarrollo sostenible. Sociedades humanas, grandes carnívoros y grandes herbívoros salvajes" - Máster en Espacios Naturales Protegidos, módulo 3 Desarrollo sostenible y servicios ambientales (coordinador Profesor Catedrático António Goméz Sal, Vice-Rector de la Universidad) - Universidad Autónoma de Madrid, Universidad Complutense de Madrid, Universidad de Alcalá, Fundación Fernando González Bernáldez, EUROPARC España - Alcalá de Henares, España - pp. 35-38.

Galhano Alves, J.P. & Harouna, Ali (2005). "Human Societies, Lions and Biodiversity in West Africa. The example of Niger W National Park region (East Gourma)" - Selección de Textos, Máster en Espacios Naturales Protegidos, módulo 3 Desarrollo sostenible y servicios ambientales (coordinador Profesor Catedrático António Goméz Sal, Vice-Rector de la Universidad) - Universidad Autónoma de Madrid, Universidad Complutense de Madrid, Universidad de Alcalá, Fundación Fernando González Bernáldez, EUROPARC España - Alcalá de Henares, España, 4 p.

Galhano Alves, J.P. (2003). "Biodiversidad total y desarrollo sostenible. Sociedades humanas, grandes carnívoros y grandes herbívoros salvajes. Nuevos conceptos para la investigación y para la acción. Dos estudios de caso: lobos en Portugal, tigres en la India" - Título de Postgrado de Especialista en Espacios Naturales Protegidos, módulo III Desarrollo sostenible y servicios ambientales (coordinador Profesor Catedrático António Goméz Sal, Vice-Rector de la Universidad) - Universidad Autónoma de Madrid, Universidad Complutense de Madrid, Universidad de Alcalá, Fundación Fernando González Bernáldez, EUROPARC España - Alcalá de Henares, España - pp. 49-51.

Galhano Alves, J.P. (2001). " Relaciones entre el hombre y la biodiversidad natural: los grandes carnívoros" - Título de Postgrado de Especialista en Espacios Naturales Protegidos, módulo III Desarrollo sostenible y servicios ambientales (coordinador Profesor Catedrático António Goméz Sal, Vice-Rector de la Universidad) - Universidad Autónoma de Madrid, Universidad Complutense de Madrid, Universidad de Alcalá, Fundación Fernando González Bernáldez, EUROPARC España - Alcalá de Henares, España - pp. 25-27.

Galhano Alves, J.P. (2001). "Les niveaux de perception de la nature et des sociétés humaines. Quelques notes méthodologiques concernant l'ethnobiologie et les sciences dont les objets d'étude se situent à l'interface de l'environnement naturel et des sociétés humaines" - Circulaire remise à des étudiants et chercheurs, Institut Agronomique Méditerranéen de Montpellier / Centre International de Hautes Études Agronomiques Méditerranéennes; Laboratoire d'Ethnobiologie-Biogéographie du Muséum National d'Histoire Naturelle – Montpellier et Paris, France - 6 p.

COLLABORATION IN COLECTIVE BOOKS

CVRVV. (2006). "Engenheiro Agrónomo Amândio Barbedo Galhano (1908-1991). Uma vida, uma causa" - Comissão de Viticultura da Região dos Vinhos Verdes; Associação Portuguesa de Horticultura; Comissão de Coordenação e Desenvolvimento Regional do Norte, Governo de Portugal - Porto, Portugal - 139 p.

Galhano Alves, J.P. & Ali Harouna. (2005). "Sociétés Humaines, lions et biodiversité en Afrique occidentale. Le cas de la région du Parc National du W du Niger (Gourma Oriental). Rapport de recherche de terrain" - 5 p - in [pp. 25, 31, 32, 34] Chardonnet, Philippe ; Crosmary, William ; Belemsobgo, Urbain ; Koulangna, Denis ; Nowell, Kristin (élaboration). (2005). "Conservation du Lion d'Afrique de l'Ouest et d'Afrique Centrale. Documents de référence pour l'atelier de Douala, Cameroun, octobre 2005" - Fondation IGF ; IUCN, SSC Cat Specialist Group, African Lion Working Group; Wildlife Conservation Society; Africa Resources Trust ; SCI Foundation ; Department for Environment, Food and Rural Affairs; Southern African Development Community - Douala, Cameroun - 116 p.

Galhano Alves, J.P. (1994). "Les Baldios" - in Politiques Foncières et Aménagements des Structures Agricoles dans les Pays Méditerranéens. Communications, complément - Çukurova University & Centre International de Hautes Études Agronomiques Méditerranéennes - Adana, Turkey et Paris, France - 15 p.

Binson, E. ; Imarazene, R. ; Galhano Alves, J.P.; Kraishi, K. et Alvar Bestilleiro, M. (1993). "Les Néo-Ruraux, Difficultés d'Implantation en Ardèche" - in Étude du Milieu Rural à l'Echelle Regionale. Le Canton des Vans (Ardèche). Rapport de Stage - Centre International de Hautes Études Agronomiques Méditerranéennes / Institut Agronomique Méditerranéen de Montpellier - Montpellier, France - 10 p.

RESEARCH PROJECTS TEXTS

Galhano Alves ; J.P. ; ONG BAIL Biodiversité et Appui aux Initiatives Locales ; Ministère du Tourisme et de l'Artisanat, République du Niger. (2009). "Projet de revalorisation de la chasse à l'arc traditionnel chez les gourmantchés en périphérie du Parc W du Niger" - ONG BAIL Biodiversité et Appui aux Initiatives Locales ; Ministère du Tourisme et de l'Artisanat, République du Niger – Niamey, Niger – 11 p.

PROSPECTUS AND CATALOGUES OF SCIENTIFIC EXHIBITONS

Galhano Alves, J.P. (2010). "Anthropologie et écosystèmes. Vivre en biodiversité totale avec des lions, tigres ou loups. Niger – Inde – Portugal" – Musée National Boubou Hama du Niger – Niamey, Niger – 16 p.

Galhano Alves, J.P. ; Cánovas, Cristina; Palacios, Fernando. (2010). "Vivir en biodiversidad total con leones, tigres o lobos" – Museo Nacional de Ciencias Naturales; Consejo Superior de Investigaciones Científicas; Fundación Biodiversidad, Ministerio de Medio Ambiente y Medio Rural y Marino; Ministerio de Ciencia e Innovación – Madrid, España – 2 p.

Galhano Alves, J.P. (2009). "Viver com leões. A coexistência entre sociedades humanas e a biodiversidade no Níger. A civilização Gourmantché" – in "Materiais diversos. Antropologias no terreno. Exposição colectiva" - CRIA (Centro em Rede de Investigação em Antropologia), Município de Miranda do Douro, Museu da Terra de Miranda, Universidade de Trás-os-Montes e Alto Douro – Lisboa & Miranda do Douro, Portugal - p. 15.

Galhano Alves, J.P.; Palacios, Fernando. (2006). "Pueblos que viven con leones, tigres o lobos. Coexistencia entre sociedades humanas y biodiversidad en Níger, India y Península Ibérica. Importancia de la gran fauna en la conservación. Exposición pública basada en los trabajos de instituciones de investigación y organizaciones de los cinco continentes" - Museo Nacional de Ciencias Naturales - Consejo Superior de Investigaciones Científicas, Ministerio de Educación y Ciencia, Gobierno de España - Madrid, España - 20 p.

OTHER PUBLICATIONS

Galhano Alves, J.P. & Wali, Soumaïla Mordia. (2004). "Une réserve de la biosphère pour tous. Randonnées dans la savane du W parmi lions et éléphants avec des guides villageois expérimentés" - Édition des auteurs - Niamey, Niger - 1 p.

CRITIC OF PUBLICATIONS IN THE MEDIAS

2009. "Un ancien étudiant de l'IAMM publie The Artificial Simulacrum World" (Galhano Alves, JP. 2009) – Lettre d'Information de l'IAMM, n° 18 (septembre-octobre 2009), Centre International de Hautes Études Méditerranéennes / Institut Agronomique Méditerranéen de Montpellier - Montpellier, France - 1 p.

2006. " El naturalista Luis del Riego publica "Contos y cuentos de lobos" (Riego Celada, Luís del; Galhano Alves, J.P. (prefacio de Ramón Grande del Brío). 2006) - La Opinión de Zamora, El Correo de Zamora, 21 de Noviembre del 2006 - Zamora, España – 1 p.

2003. "Vivre en Biodiversité Totale. Des hommes, des grands carnivores et des grands herbivores sauvages. Deux études de cas : loups au Portugal, tigres en Inde" (Galhano Alves, JP. 2002) - La Voie du Loup, nº 15, Mission Loup, France Nature Environnement (Fédération Française des Associations de Protection de la Nature et de l'Environnement) - Paris, France - p. 6.

2002. "Vivre en Biodiversité Totale. Des hommes, des grands carnivores et des grands herbivores sauvages. Deux études de cas : loups au Portugal, tigres en Inde" (Galhano Alves, JP. 2002) - @dam News, nº 22 (mars 2002) - http:// adam.mmsh.univ-aix.fr), Association d'Anthropologie Méditerranéenne (ADAM), Maison Méditerranéenne des Sciences de l'Homme, Université d'Aix-Marseille - Aix-en-Provence, France.

INTERVIEWS TO THE MEDIAS

Localvisão TV - Bragança (2014). Jornadas de Identidade Rural organizadas pela ZOELA com o intuito de preservar ruralidade – 15-11-2014 – Bragança, Portugal.

Television Dounia (2010). "Pedro Galhano. Un chercheur portugais au Niger" – Programme "Patrimoine " – 23-11-2010 – 10h30-11h00 (avec rediffusions successives en novembre et décembre 2010, et en 2014 par d'autres Télévisions du Niger) – Niamey, Niger.

Radio Nacional de España - Radio 3. (2007). "Mesa redonda sobre prácticas y tradición oral del lobo, y conservación de la especie, en España y Portugal" - Programa Trebede -Participantes: Galhano Alves, J.P.; Horacio; Peña, Iñaki (entrevistador); Riego Celada, Luis del - 20-2-2007 - 20h00-21h00 - Madrid, España.

Nunes, Maria Leonor. (2004). "Galhano Alves. Guardador de mundos. Um bicho antropológico" - JL Jornal de Letras, Artes e Ideias, Ano XXIV / nº 882, 21 Julho a 3 Agosto 2004 - Paço de Arcos, Portugal - p. 25.

Rus, Aurora (texto); Sierra, Jorge (fotos). (2002). "Tigre de Bengala. Entre la mitología y la extinción" - La Tierra que todos desearíamos, Publicación medioambiental, S.L., Verano 2002 - Madrid, España - pp. 48-60.

Note : avec un article écrit par moi, complémentaire à l'interview, p. 60.

Gatinho, Helena. (2001). "Um mundo perfeito" - Expresso, secção Vidas, 21-7-2001 - Portugal, p. 40.

Garcias, Pedro. (2001). "Do lobo de Montesinho ao tigre de Sariska, na Índia" - Público, secção Terra, 21-4-200 - Portugal - p. 39.

Rodríguez, Eusebio. (2000). "Sanabria - La Carballeda. Joao Pedro Galhano, antropólogo: mantener las estructuras agrarias favorece al ecosistema" - La Opinión de Zamora, 11-12-2000 - Zamora, España - p. 18.

Televisión de Zamora, Castilla León. (2000). Entrevista sobre la conservación del lobo y de la biodiversidad - 9-12-2000 - Zamora, España.

REFERENCES OF MY RESEARCH WORKS IN ENCYCLOPEDIAS

fr.wikipedia.org - Français – Gourmantché (peuple)
en.wikipedia.org - English - Gurma people
pt.frwiki.wiki - Português – Gourmantché (pessoas)
Wikiwand - África - Gurma

fr.wikipedia.org - Français – Gurjar (tribu)

fr.wikipedia.org – Français - Propriété foncière
fr.wikipedia.org – Français - Foncier
en.wikipedia.org – English - Land (economics)
en.wikipedia.org – English - Common land

The author writes also litterature, prose and poetry, and he published yet two novels and five books of poetry, in Portuguese and in Portugal, among other publications in Portugal and Brazil.